Breaking Free From Lo

After working as a research
department of a Zulu hospital, Helena Wilkinson trained
in counselling. For four years she was the Editor of *Carer
and Counsellor*. She is the author of six books and
numerous booklets, and is a member of the Society of
Authors and the Society of Women Writers and Journal-
ists. Helena was the Founder of Kainos Trust for eating
disorders, and operated as Director until January 2004
when she joined the full-time team of Nicholaston House,
a Christian healing centre on Gower, attached to Swansea
City Mission.

Unless otherwise stated all biblical quotations are taken from the Good News Bible.

Other books by Helena Wilkinson published by RoperPenberthy Publishing Ltd. are:

Beyond Chaotic Eating
Puppet on a String

BREAKING FREE FROM LONELINESS

HELENA WILKINSON

RoperPenberthy Publishing Ltd
Horsham, England

Published by RoperPenberthy Publishing Ltd
PO Box 545, Horsham, England RH12 4QW

Text copyright © Helena Wilkinson 2004

First published in Great Britain in 1997
by Hodder & Stoughton Ltd
Updated version published by
RoperPenberthy Publishing Ltd 2004

ISBN 1 903905 19 2

Cover design by Angie Moyler

Typeset by Avocet Typeset, Chilton, Aylesbury, Bucks
Printed in the United Kingdom by Cox & Wyman Ltd,
Reading, Berkshire

CONTENTS

Contents

INTRODUCTION

The following introduction was written when *Breaking Free From Loneliness* was initially published in 1996. I feel these words are still valid and hence I have chosen to leave them as they stand rather than write another introduction.

Do you know that breaking free from loneliness is possible or have you been led to believe that it's something you have to endure until circumstances change for the better?

I believe that loneliness is something to be overcome, not endured. Some people will teach you that loneliness is inevitable and that it's necessary to accept it as part of the legacy of the fall of mankind (spoken of in Genesis 3).

Whilst I accept that the world we live in isn't perfect or free from struggles, I don't believe that we have to learn to live with loneliness. On the other hand, this doesn't mean that we have to be unrealistic in saying that we never feel lonely. We all have moments of loneliness but this is very different from the experience of deep and ongoing loneliness.

As my belief is that you can overcome loneliness I felt that it was important to write a book which you'll find is very different from other books on the subject. The focus throughout this book is on *freedom from*, and not being *comforted in*, loneliness. Whilst some of the chapter titles are ones that you can probably relate to in the midst of your struggles, the text of the book directs you towards breaking free.

Being directed towards freedom from a problem is quite different from being comforted in a problem. I remember a very difficult time in my life when I was faced with a painful past situation. I chose to hold on to what had happened in order to receive the comfort I needed. I sought answers that fed my desire for comfort, but the result was drastic; I experienced deeper pain, became more distanced from God and carried out behaviour patterns contrary to God's ways. I began to wonder if I would ever be free. I then reached a place where I became desperate enough to listen to a totally different approach: focusing on God's solution and not my solution. I chose to seek the truth of God's word and not the comfort of my own feelings. This approach hurt, but it was a different kind of pain. It was no longer a desperate pain but a growing pain.

As you read *Breaking Free From Loneliness* you may find that at times it causes a reaction in you. You want words of comfort and someone to understand. When you find that this isn't happening your natural reaction is to close the book and say that it's 'too spiritual' or 'the author doesn't understand'. At this point be brave enough to open the book again and discover that God's truth brings life, whilst merely seeking comfort creates a void which you may not realise incorporates loneliness.

The more you fill the void with 'things' the less you think you'll experience loneliness but in fact you find that it's a bottomless pit and loneliness still lurks. As one attempt after another fails, and one year fades into another, despondency sets in: can you – and will you – ever be free? Yes you can! The path to freedom is through learning about, and applying, God's principles. It's my desire and my payer that as some of those principles are presented in this book you'll choose to put them into operation and break free from loneliness.

In order to help this process you'll notice that at the end of each chapter there is a 'Truth' and an 'Action' section. I have purposely put the 'Truth' section first because it's important to focus on the truth. The 'Action' section follows so that you can choose to put into operation the principles arising from the truth. Whatever order you read the chapters in, pray that as you read them you'll receive a revelation of the truth. Breaking free from loneliness doesn't happen as a result of merely applying a formula but as a result of revelation from God.

May God bless you and bring you lasting freedom.

Helena Wilkinson
Nicholaston House,
Penmaen, Gower, Swansea, 2004

1 | *WHY ARE YOU LONELY?*

Do you know why you are lonely? Perhaps, like many people, you don't know the answer to that question, or if you do, the answer still doesn't take away the pain and the feeling.

It can be helpful to realise that there are essentially two different types of loneliness: *circumstantial loneliness* and *the state of loneliness*. Circumstantial loneliness is experienced in response to a change in circumstances, e.g. losing someone close or being without company for a period of time. Generally we know when we're feeling lonely as a result of circumstances, and we know what is needed to bring a change even if we don't have the resources to implement that change.

The state of loneliness is more complex because it's as a result of various factors, both emotional and spiritual, and it becomes a way of life. If you don't know why you're lonely then you'll almost certainly be in a state of loneliness. You may not be able to make a connection between your past experiences, the way you relate or where you are spiritually with the fact that you're feeling lonely. As you become aware of one aspect of your loneliness and endeavour to resolve it, you can be left wondering why you still feel so alone because you may believe that there is a single cause. However, for most people in a state of loneliness several aspects of their lives need to be dealt with before the deep and often crippling feelings go.

The word 'crippling' aptly describes the state of loneliness for many, because to them it feels as though it disables their lives. You can liken it to being trapped in a deep pit which has tunnels leading to dead ends. All around is space and each echo of one's own voice acts as a crushing reminder of the hollowness and the desolation. As times passes by it creeps deep into your innermost being and its poison takes hold through lack of bonding, not feeling accepted and not belonging. The experience leaves you feeling weak, vulnerable, powerless and trapped, with no way out.

There is a way out and it starts by unravelling all the different factors which go to make up your state of loneliness. If you don't begin to unravel the different factors, and to address them, your state of loneliness actually ends up making you feel even more isolated and alone. Although these factors may be unique to each individual, the following is a list of a few which I consider relevant. Some of these may feel very real to you. They, along with many others, will be explored in greater detail throughout the book. I suggest that to help you identify the reasons behind *your* loneliness, you look at these factors in the light of the question 'Do I':

- find it difficult to express my feelings or even know what my feelings are?
- feel empty of meaningful friendships?
- have high expectations of myself and others, and quickly feel let down or disappointed?
- find open and direct communication very painful or difficult?
- think that other people always seem to be coping when I'm not?
- find it difficult to assert myself and set boundaries such as saying 'no' when I mean 'no'?
- feel raw and vulnerable and in need of protecting myself from further wounds?
- present a different image on the outside from how I feel on the inside?

- often feel misunderstood, and yet unable to change the way some people view me?
- think that I'm different and always feel that I'm 'on the outside'?
- feel overcome by fears of aloneness, rejection and not being valued?
- want someone to rescue me from difficult situations believing that I can't help myself?
- feel that I don't have the resources to fight a continuous battle?
- feel empty on the inside, even if my life is full of activity and people?
- still feel that I'm a victim of painful past experiences?
- still sense that I'm searching spiritually, or that even though I have faith in God it doesn't seem enough to take away my loneliness?

There is a way out for each and every factor you face. It may seem at this stage that what lies before you is a mass of tangled briers, but with God's help you can be free. I know from personal experience the pain of loneliness but I also know the freedom from loneliness. Right from the beginning of your journey learn to cry out to God for help. He is beside you, walking with you every step of the way, wanting to bring you to that place of freedom. Let Him gradually take you there and watch the changes taking place.

Truth

> Show me your ways, O Lord,
> teach me your paths;
> guide me in your truth and teach me,
> for you are God my Saviour,
> and my hope is in you all day long.
> (Psalm 25:4–5)

Action

1. Pray the above passage from the Bible and, as you do so, use it as a heart cry to God to help you in overcoming your loneliness.
2. Start to become aware of all the different factors behind your loneliness. If it's helpful to do so, write these down and tell God about them, asking Him to help you face them.
3. Make the decision to do whatever it takes to be free and ask God to give you a real desire for a 'loneliness-free' life.

2 | HOW STRONG ARE YOUR ROOTS?

If the state of loneliness is made up of many different factors where do you begin in breaking free from loneliness? The first step is having a desire for new life: a life without the chains which bind you to feeling lonely on the inside, even if there are people around.

One way I would illustrate this is to liken our new life to a plant's new life. As a young plant grows it's vital that it develops good roots. So too, if we are going to find a new 'loneliness-free' life we need to develop good roots.

Although there are different kinds of roots the most important, and the first to aim to establish, are the spiritual roots. Many people have put down spiritual roots in their lives but they are ineffective. Others have put down roots but they can't grow because, like a plant restrained in too small a pot, they are restrained by their lack of understanding of how God sets us free.

How strong are *your* roots? If the roots of a plant are weak, the plant is vulnerable. Do you want to be free from vulnerability? If you do, then it's necessary to look at the most basic and essential roots for good growth. We need to understand that:

1. Our sense of emptiness originates in our separation from God.
2. Our only way back to God is through Jesus, because of what was accomplished through Jesus' death.
3. In order for Jesus' death to impact our lives sufficiently to free us from loneliness we need to be in relationship with Him.

4. Our means of being able to apply to our lives what has been accomplished through Jesus, is through the Holy Spirit.

Let's look at each of these in turn in more detail. As we do so, stop and ask yourself if you need to put down firmer roots in any of these areas.

1. *Our sense of emptiness originates in our separation from God.*

In the opening chapter of Genesis, the very beginning of the Bible, we read how God created the heavens and the earth, and how He created the first man and woman, Adam and Eve. Genesis 1 tells us that man was made in the image of God. His eyes had not been opened to sin and so he lived in perfection and in total security with God. God was everything to him and met his every need. However, there was one commandment which God gave to man: 'You are free to eat from any tree in the garden, but you must not eat from the tree of the knowledge of good and evil, for when you eat of it you will surely die' (Genesis 2:16, 17).

What followed was Satan putting doubt into Eve's mind concerning what God had said. 'You will not surely die ... For God knows that when you eat of it your eyes will be opened, and you will be like God, knowing good and evil' (Genesis 3:4–5). As a result Adam and Eve disobeyed God and ate the fruit. The consequence of their sin was separation from Him.

Imagine having your every need met and having security in God and then being separated from Him, with no way back. The inner emptiness and longing for needs to be met must have been excruciating. It's the same inner emptiness and feeling of unmet needs which we now feel, and which only God can satisfy.

Adam and Eve's separation from God resulted in mankind's separation from Him. We could not be in His presence because, being imperfect, sin caused a division. Whilst God remained holy, mankind became unholy.

2. *Our only way back to God is through Jesus, because of what was accomplished through Jesus' death.*
In order to be acceptable in God's sight, therefore no longer separated from Him and no longer empty, there needed to be a bridge between God and us. The first Adam caused separation and so God sent His only Son, Jesus, as the second Adam to bridge the gap of separation. Jesus came to this earth both fully human *and* fully divine so He could be the link between us and God. Had there not been a human and a perfect sacrifice for our sins the sacrifice would have been meaningless. Jesus' blood now stands between us and God, enabling us to be acceptable in His sight.

3. *In order for Jesus' death to impact our lives sufficiently to free us from loneliness we need to be in relationship with Him.*
Whilst it is the blood of Jesus which closes the gap between God and us, we have actually to *receive* the blood of Jesus. This means that we have to believe that Jesus is the Son of God: that He died as our sacrifice and He now stands between us and God. It's like being given a new outfit to wear; you only see the effect when you actually put the garment on. To look at the garment and say that it exists is not sufficient. It has to be worn! In the same way we have to be 'clothed in the blood of Jesus': that is, we have to receive Jesus as Lord over our lives.

When we receive Jesus as Lord, God looks at us *through* Jesus. Because we are now clothed in Jesus' blood, God sees Jesus in us and He sees Jesus' righteousness and holiness.

When we claim Jesus' Lordship over us we have the same resources as Jesus. Imagine putting on your new garment and walking around in it but not knowing what it's worth or what's in the pockets. Even though you have a new outfit it doesn't seem to make that much difference to the way you view yourself or how others see you. It's a garment and nothing more. All the time you remain unaware that the pockets are filled with riches which provide you with everything you'll ever need in life. We have a wealth of resources in Jesus, but until we know them we can't use them.

4. *Our means of being able to apply to our lives what has been accomplished through Jesus, is through the Holy Spirit.*
If your new garment had come with an instruction manual which told you of the treasures inside the pockets, you would want to understand those instructions; it would be difficult if they were written in a language which was unfamiliar. The Holy Spirit is our instructor who gives us the power to apply the teaching. We may have an instructor but unless we allow him to teach us we remain none the wiser. In the same way we must accept the Holy Spirit and be filled with Him continuously. The Holy Spirit:

- creates (Genesis 1:1–2)
- reveals (Ezekiel 37:1–2)
- convicts (Psalm 51:10–12)
- has skill, ability and knowledge (Exodus 31:1–3)
- transforms (1 Samuel 10:6)
- has power (1 Samuel 16:13)
- is the giver of gifts (Romans 12:6–8)

Truth

Jesus said, 'I have come that they may have life, and have it to the full.'

(John 10:10)

Action

1. If your roots aren't strong and firm ask God to help you strengthen them.
2. If you haven't given your life to Jesus acknowledge before Him that you have gone your own way but no longer want to. Ask Jesus to be Lord of your life and see yourself clothed in His blood; acceptable before God.
3. If you have not received the Holy Spirit, ask God to baptise you in, and fill you with, His Spirit.

3 | MEETING OUR LONGINGS

In the last chapter we saw how we have been created to have our deep inner needs met by God. Perhaps the greatest of these is the longing to be loved; to be special and to be significant in the eyes of another person. If these longings aren't met then there is often disappointment, loss and emptiness. We look at other people and they appear to have what we believe will make the difference. They have confidence, friendships, marriage, significant roles, etc. We also believe that we can't be happy and without loneliness unless our circumstances change, believing that if they do then we'll be able to 'give more of ourselves to God'. This is not so – true happiness comes from being filled from the inside and not being changed on the outside.

We all have three levels of longings – physical, emotional and spiritual – but have a tendency to concentrate on the physical and emotional longings. It can be helpful to see your longings in terms of circles. Take a piece of paper and draw a small circle within a large circle. The small circle represents your spiritual longings whilst the large outer circle represents your emotional and physical longings. Colour in the outer circle leaving the inner one blank. It doesn't matter how technicoloured the outer circle is, if the inner circle is still blank it remains empty. Even if you colour in the outer circle and go over the line a little into the inner circle, the core still remains untouched. It is the core which needs to be filled in order to be free from inner emptiness. This is the part which only God, through Jesus, can meet.

If we truly want our longings to be met we must concentrate on filling this inner circle. If you throw a stone into a pond the stone is in the centre and the ripples radiate out. If the spiritual longings are met they radiate out and profoundly touch the emotional and physical aspects of our lives.

How do you have your spiritual longings met? How does the inner circle begin to fill up? They can only be met in relationship with God, but you aren't going to have a relationship with Him until you know His character. Like any relationship you have to get to know the person and what he/she is like before you trust that person and allow him/her to draw close to you. When we know the character of God, we begin to understand the essentials about our own identity because not only do we know the nature of the Giver but we know the nature of His gifts.

What is the giver like? He is a God who:

- is gracious and compassionate, slow to anger and rich in love (Psalm 145:8)
- is faithful and just if we confess our sins and will purify us from all unrighteousness (1 John 1:9)
- is rich in mercy (Ephesians 2:4)
- can do all things (Job 42:2)
- is the giver of every good and perfect gift (James 1:17)
- is holy and awesome (Psalm 111:9)
- is the rock, whose works are perfect and all His ways just (Deuteronomy 32:4)
- is strong and mighty (Psalm 24:8)
- is holy and whose glory fills the whole earth (Isaiah 6:3)
- is glorious and majestic (Psalm 111:3)
- is the same yesterday, today and for ever (Hebrews 13:8)

Some of the Hebrew names for God might also help you to understand more about the nature of Him:

- Yireh: provider (Genesis 22:14)
- Rophe: healer (Psalm 103:3)
- M'kedesh: sanctifier (Ephesians 1:4)
- Nissi: banner (Exodus 17:15)
- Rohi: shepherd (Psalm 23:1)
- Shalom: peace (Judges 6:24)
- Tsidkenu: righteousness (Jeremiah 23:6)
- Shammah: ever present (Deuteronomy 31:6)
- El Shaddi: all sufficient (Genesis 49:25)

Because God has called us to be in relationship with Him we need to proclaim over ourselves the truth about who God is in relation to us. He is our:

- provider
- healer
- sanctifier
- banner
- shepherd
- peace
- righteousness

We can sometimes struggle with believing or seeing the evidence of God as our healer and provider. Our struggles prevent us from accepting these parts of His character. Whilst we can't always understand God's ways, if we want to know the reality of His different attributes and the relevance of them to our lives, a good place to start is by proclaiming them. Proclaiming means speaking something out. For instance, you may say aloud 'God is rich in mercy' or 'God You are very gracious' or 'Your word says that you are my provider and so I thank you that You will provide for my every need'. As we speak out words about who God is our faith increases and we move from a place of saying God is our provider, because the Bible tells us He is, to believing He is our provider and then experiencing Him as our provider.

Truth

My souls find rest in God alone; my salvation comes
from Him. He alone is my rock and my salvation; He is
my fortress, I shall never be shaken.

(Psalm 62:1–2)

Action

1. Spend time reading about the nature of God.
2. Start proclaiming over yourself that God is your shepherd, your peace, your provider, etc.
3. If you struggle over believing or knowing God's provi-
   sion and/or healing in your life, ask God to show you
   these in a very practical way.

4 | WHERE IS OUR SECURITY?

One of the main reasons for being lonely is to do with where our security is placed. If our security is in people, ourselves, our circumstances, or life, then when there's a change in any one of these things there's a change in our security. It's therefore vital that our security is based on the right foundation. But in a world which is full of choices how do we know what the right foundation is? And does the foundation really make that much difference? Jesus spoke clearly about foundations when He told the parable about the wise and foolish builder.

> Therefore everyone who hears these words of mine and puts them into practice is like a wise man who built his house on the rock. The rain came down, the streams rose, and the winds blew and beat against the house; yet it did not fall, because it had its foundation on the rock. But everyone who hears these words of mine and does not put them into practice is like a foolish man who built his house on sand. The rain came down, the streams rose, and the winds blew and beat against that house, and it fell with a great crash.
>
> (Matthew 7:24–27)

We may have a world full of choices but only one foundation lasts through the storms and that is a life built not only upon belief in Jesus, but by putting into practice His words on a daily basis. Why is this so important? Because God know that when we put the words of Jesus into practice it automatically creates security. As soon as we don't put them into practice (and we are all good at doing that!) we start to draw on other things in order to feel secure. We draw on our relationship with others, our success, career, status, finances, etc. Each of these becomes a pocket of security for us but because they change with the tide of life, just like the sand, they have no lasting foundation. They only create security as long as they are going well.

Do you want a life of stability which is not shaken by the turbulent winds in life? Psalm 125:1 says 'Those who trust in the Lord are like Mount Zion, which cannot be shaken but endures for ever'. Notice the psalmist does not say those who *believe* in the Lord cannot be shaken, but those who *trust* in the Lord. You believe in the faithfulness and trustworthiness of God because of what His word says about Him, not because of your experience of Him. We can easily assume that if God doesn't answer our prayers He can't be trusted. Our confidence must be in *who* God is, not what He does for us. If we look to His acts and not to His character our security goes up and down according to whether 'He has done anything' that day. I also find that knowing God as my security means seeing myself standing on the rock and not the sand. Whether I am feeling secure or not at that moment I still need to declare that God is my security.

I find that an essential part of knowing God as my security in everyday situations is to remind myself of the parable of the rock and the sand. Even if I'm feeling shaky I can still thank God that He is my security. As I reaffirm this to myself and realise that He doesn't change, I find myself becoming more and more secure.

You may be feeling that you don't know what to say to God or how to declare to Him that He is your security. When we don't know what to say to Him it is good to speak aloud chunks of Scripture as a prayer. As we do this the words in Scripture actually teach us what God is like and how to trust Him. Try reading these verses from

Psalm 103 aloud several times. Before you read them ask God to work in you deeply to create security, because only He can bring about such a change. As you do so note how you begin to feel better! God's truth never fails and always bring life to us.

> Praise the Lord, O my soul;
> all my inmost being, praise his holy name.
> Praise the Lord, O my soul,
> and forget not all his benefits -
> who forgives all your sins
> and heals all your diseases,
> who redeems your life from the pit
> and crowns you with life and compassion,
> who satisfies your desires with good things
> so that your youth is renewed like the eagle's...
> The Lord is compassionate and gracious,
> slow to anger, abounding in love.
> He will not always accuse, nor will he harbour his anger
>   for ever;
> he does not treat us as our sins deserve
> or repay us according to our iniquities.
> For as high as the heavens are above the earth,
> so great is his love for those who fear him;
> as far as the east is from the west,
> so far has he removed our transgressions from us.

As we speak out all the truths about who God is to us it is as if we gain a real purity and freshness. Imagine having blood poisoning and all the toxins floating around your bloodstream are causing you to feel extremely rough. The blood poisoning is like all the insecurities in your life. How did the blood become poisoned? By all the impurities of failed relationships, hurts, disappointments, and negative thoughts, etc. Unless the toxins are destroyed and your blood is made pure you will continue to feel bad and in your rough state feel so terribly alone.

The pure blood is like an infusion of God's truth which is His written word, the Bible. The Bible tells us who God is, who we are in relation to God, and how to live in freedom. If you reject treatment for blood poisoning you remain feeling rough; but if you accept treatment you receive new life. In the same way if we reject, or don't put into practice, God's truth we remain with a fluctuating security.

If you want a stable security, effectively you need a blood transfusion! In order for this to take place you not only need to ask God to help you but you also need to read and apply different aspects of the truth. A good place to begin is to read the book of Ephesians.

Truth

The eternal God is your refuge, and underneath are the everlasting arms.

(Deuteronomy 33:27)

Action

1. Picture God as your refuge, and His arms underneath you so that you cannot fall other than into His love and compassion.
2. As you enter into relationship with God, praising him, ask Him to create a deep change in you whereby He becomes your security. You are totally secure with Him.
3. Start affirming aloud the fact that your security is in God.

5 | OUR IDENTITY IN GOD

One aspect of the truth is the truth about who you are as a child of God. Do you ever feel you are different and 'on the outside'? Do you perceive this difference as negative which causes you a lot of pain, leaving you in a state of loneliness? How you feel about yourself in relation to others can often contribute to loneliness. The person who has a strong sense of their identity isn't the person who struggles with the inner ache of loneliness. If, however, there are weak points in your belief about your identity, relationships have the tendency to be fragile and self-doubt can easily overwhelm you.

When you don't feel good about yourself you can't give of yourself. Instead you expect the worst, feel left out and end up trying to take from people in order to make up for how you feel. Rather than doing this, the answer is to learn more about your true identity. This is often the point at which people get stuck: they know what that means and how it should impact their lives. They don't know that the search for their identity ended at the point when they gave their lives to Jesus because at that point they received their identity in Christ.

What does 'our identity is in Christ' mean? In the New Testament the apostle Paul mentions that 'we are in Christ' and that 'Christ is in us', indicating that it is Jesus' life which gives us our essential identity. Most people when asked to describe themselves talk about culture, social standing, heritage, family background, etc. Paul goes on to say that none of this applies any more because our identity is no longer determined by these factors: our identity lies in the fact that we are children of God. We are no longer products of our past: we are essentially products of what was accomplished through Jesus' life, death and resurrection.

The truth about you is that you:

- are God's child (Romans 8:16)
- are in Christ Jesus (1 Corinthians 1:30)
- are Christ's friend (John 15:15)
- have been bought at a price (1 Corinthians 6:20)
- are a new creation, the old has gone, the new has come (2 Corinthians 5:17)
- were chosen in Christ before the creation of the world (Ephesians 1:4)
- are God's chosen one, holy and dearly loved (Colossians 3:12)
- are one of Christ's ambassadors (2 Corinthians 5:20)
- are God's workmanship (Ephesians 2:10)
- have been blessed with every spiritual blessing in Christ (Ephesians 1:3)
- have been given a spirit of power, of love and of self-discipline (2 Timothy 1:7)
- have been given fullness in Christ (Colossians 2:10)

Another essential part of our identity is what has been accomplished for us through the cross and blood of Jesus. The Bible tells us we:

- have been saved by grace through faith (Ephesians 2:8)
- have been rescued from the dominion of darkness and brought into the kingdom of God's Son (Colossians 1:13)
- have been reconciled to God through Jesus (Colossians 1:22)
- have been born again of imperishable seed (1 Peter 1:23)
- have been given eternal life (1 John 5:11)
- have direct access to God through the Holy Spirit (Ephesians 2:18)

- cannot be separated from the love of God (Romans 8:35)
- are free from condemnation (Romans 8:1)

We need no longer feel 'on the outside', a nobody, lost and alone. Instead we can speak with confidence of where we have come from, where we are going and the essentials about our identity. However, we only experience a greater sense of freedom from the burden of 'feeling a nobody' if we actually apply God's word to ourselves.

The truth about us remains the same whether we say we can't believe it and don't deserve it, or whether we accept that it is true despite how we feel. Imagine someone buys you a new car, gives you the keys and leaves it in your drive. The car has been given to you and it belongs to you. If you can't believe it's yours and so you don't drive it this doesn't alter the fact of your ownership. Why let unbelief and guilt prevent you from enjoying what you have been given, when you could be driving around and making the most of it!

In the same way, even if we can't believe our identity is in Christ it does not change the fact that our identity in Him exists! The truth remains the same whether we apply it to our lives or not but if we don't apply it we cannot reap the benefits and consequently our stability is affected. Why search for an identity when you have one waiting to be claimed? Why search for answers when you have *the* answer?

Truth

> You were taught with regard to your former way of life to put off your old self… to be made new in the attitude of your minds; and to put on the new self, created to be like God in true righteousness and holiness.
>
> (Ephesians 4:22–24)

Action

1. Write out the truths about who you are as God's child and personalise them: 'I am God's chosen one, holy and dearly loved', etc.
2. Read these truths over yourself each day and thank God that they are for you personally.
3. Ask God to help you to accept any truths which you find difficult to believe.

6 | MOUNTAINS CAN MOVE

When one day of loneliness merges into another it's easy to feel that other people have given up on you, and it's even easier to give up on yourself. God does not give up on any of us and for this reason we must not give up on ourselves either.

We have looked at the importance of believing God's word above our own thoughts and words, so if God says He is faithful and just we must believe He will see us through our experiences, including loneliness. There is a spiritual principle behind speaking out the truth. For instance, if you say 'there's no point trying' you are effectively saying that nothing can change, and yet the truth of God's word declares '… with God all things are possible' (Matthew 19:26). When you declare that 'all things are possible' your faith increases and you can start to pray, believing that things will change. It is by our faith that we see the 'mountains' in our lives removed.

Although things may look black we still need to speak life and to see beyond our situation. It's also important to see beyond our feelings, which can so easily lead us to speak negatively. We don't look at a tree in winter and say that it can't bear fruit because it has no leaves! As spring emerges and summer develops, we see leaves and fruit, not empty branches!

In Deuteronomy we read of being given two options: life and death.

> See, I set before you today life and prosperity, death and destruction. For I command you today to love the Lord

your God, to walk in His ways, and to keep his commands, decrees and laws; then you will live and increase, and the Lord your God will bless you in the land you are entering to possess.

But if your heart turns away and you are not obedient ... you will certainly be destroyed ... I have set before you life and death, blessings and curses. Now choose life, so that you and your children may live.

(Deuteronomy 30:15–19)

So many people have no idea that each time they say negative things about themselves, situations or others, they can actually bring destruction into their lives. Words have immense power, especially spiritually. I remember when I was at Bible College being told about an incident of a man who was in a financial crisis. He also had something wrong with his foot which was causing him a lot of distress. He went to see a number of doctors, who couldn't explain the situation. He frequently spoke about his financial problem but it wasn't until someone heard him say 'My mortgage is crippling me' that the connection was made between what he was saying and his current circumstances. He renounced the words 'crippling me' and immediately the problem with his foot disappeared! The story illustrates the power of the spoken word. Words which bring life to us are words which encourage, build up and result in growth. Words which bring death and destruction are words which cause doubt, fear and condemnation and result in introspection.

Why is it so important then to choose life and not death? Because it's the difference between choosing God's ways rather than Satan's ways. Satan was an angel who, after rebelling against God, was hurled out of heaven along with his followers (demons). He opposes God and hence God's ways. One of his main tactics is to prevent us from believing that God's truth can make a difference to out lives. For believers, he has no power over our lives because Jesus' death and resurrection defeated his power. The only power he now has over us is his lies. When we do not stand against his lies by believing the truth we may not realise it but we choose death, not life.

Each time we do not believe, or put into operation, what God says is true we in effect send out satellite messages saying 'attack me'. We innocently think the words don't really matter and yet at the same time the hidden message is picked up and followed through. We can't understand why we feel so pulled down and even become frustrated with God because 'He does not do anything'. Consequently we fail to act on His words 'Now choose life so that you and your children may live'.

Are you going to begin to speak blessings over yourself? Why not start by speaking about what you can now do as a result of Jesus breaking the power of Satan on the cross:

- I can approach the throne of grace with confidence (Hebrews 4:16)
- I can receive mercy and find grace to help in my time of need (Hebrews 4:16)
- I can be transformed by the renewing of my mind (Romans 12:2)
- I can do all things through Him who gives me strength (Philippians 4:13)
- By faith I can do the same works as Jesus did (John 14:12)
- My heart and mind are guarded by the peace of God (Philippians 4:7)
- There is no condemnation for me because I am in Christ Jesus (Romans 8:1)
- I am more than a conqueror through Him who loves me (Romans 8:37)
- I can overcome Satan by the blood of Jesus and the word of my testimony (Revelation 12:11)

- Greater is he that is in me than he that is in the world (1 John 4:4)

Each time you catch yourself contradicting the word of God such as 'I'm no good', shout 'stop!' Then say, 'I renounce that, it's not true. The truth says that I am more than a conqueror'. It is also enormously helpful to write down all the common things you say about yourself which do not bring life, and opposite each one to write the truth. To do this you will need to know what the truth is. You could begin by writing out all the sentences I have noted so far and see where each one fits into your life to replace the lies about you.

Never underestimate the power of your spoken words. The whole course of our well-being can be directed by the tongue!

> ... take ships as an example. Although they are so large and are driven by strong winds, they are steered by a very small rudder wherever the pilot wants to go. Likewise the tongue is a small part of the body, but it makes great boasts ... The tongue also is a fire, a world of evil among the parts of the body. It corrupts the whole person, sets the whole course of his life on fire ... With the tongue we praise our Lord and Father, and with it we curse men, who have been made in God's likeness.
>
> (James 3:4–6, 9)

If we say 'life is too difficult' or 'we might as well give up trying', and if our tongue directs the course of life, such words will lead to destruction and failure. Think before you speak!

Truth

The fear of the Lord is a fountain of life, turning a man from the snares of death.

(Proverbs 14:27)

Action

1. If you have spoken untruths about yourself, life or God, acknowledge these before God and ask for His forgiveness.
2. Make a commitment never to give up on yourself.
3. Make the decision each day to choose life, watching carefully what you say.

7 | A SENSE OF ISOLATION

Once you have a solid spiritual foundation it becomes easier both to look at and work on other issues. From my own experience I've noticed that one of the main issues behind loneliness is the struggle to express and handle emotions.

People are frequently brought up with misconceptions surrounding emotions, which consistently disrupt their lives. A classic example is that as a Christian it's wrong to be angry. In the Bible it says, 'In your anger do not sin. Do not let the sun go down while you are still angry' (Ephesians 4:26). It does not say that you cannot be angry but that you must not sin (go against God's laws) in dealing with your anger. When we sin as a result of our anger we 'give the devil a foothold' (Ephesians 4:27), to bring destruction within a situation. Once we have given the devil an opening in our lives we find that anger can quickly lead to unforgiveness, bitterness, deep hurt and emotional torment. As hard as we try, we can't get out of the cycle because it has now become a spiritual battle.

This spiritual battle, resulting in chaotic and sometimes deeply disturbing emotions, only reinforces our belief that negative emotions are wrong. Our only solution is to push these emotions down. But doing this has two consequences:

1. Emotions which are buried are buried alive not dead and will show themselves in some other form. Buried anger is often the root of depression.
2. When you numb your negative feelings part of your

positive feelings can become 'frozen' too. This can leave you feeling like an empty shell, expressionless and without personality. You can't relate to others when you feel like an empty shell, and so feel very alone.

One reason people 'numb' their feelings is often to try to survive the hurts experienced early in life. When they do this they can soon become out of touch with what feelings are. If you cannot put a name to emotions you will not recognise them when they arise. This leaves you at a loss to know what to do with them. They are always bubbling away under the surface but you don't recognise them so they are more likely to show themselves through your behaviour. That behaviour can so easily be contrary to God's ways.

As believers we are called to be led by faith and not by feelings, but we must still know what our feelings are. We must not push feelings down, neither must we let them dominate. Since feelings are an indicator of what's going on inside us, we must get a balance between listening to them but not being controlled by them. Some people can't even put words to feelings: understanding what words are appropriate can be a good place to start. If you find it difficult to know how you feel, see if you can relate to any of the following:

- disappointed
- grieving
- guilty
- agonised
- pained
- frustrated
- enraged

If your feelings are locked away ask God, in His time and in His gentleness, slowly to release your emotions. When we ask God to help us we have no need to root around deep inside ourselves, digging deeper and trying harder. Doing this can create a great deal of damage.

Once you start to know what the different feelings are, particularly the major groups

love	guilt
joy	anxiety
peace	anger
happiness	fear

you can begin to look at the inner and outer reality, and how to respond. What do I mean by inner and outer reality? Suppose you are standing on a cliff top and someone touches you on the shoulder and you experience fear. That fear is in connection with outer reality and tells you not to step forward. On the other hand a fear of rejection comes from within you.

One of the most common emotions which results in loneliness is guilt. Again guilt can be in connection with outer reality or inner reality, more commonly called true or false guilt. True guilt is a feeling which occurs when you violate a law or standard. The guilt can be dealt with through repentance and forgiveness. False guilt is when you think you are bad or wrong. It comes from within us in response to over-sensitivity, lack of worth and self-condemnation. The only way we can deal with false guilt is to recognise that it has no reality, to speak truth over ourselves and not lies, and to set realistic standards.

Guilt and feelings of rejection are often tied together and arise from ourselves and other people setting high standards. If we did not come up to people's expectations as children we take upon ourselves feelings of disapproval and inadequacy. We will crave approval, which in turn leads to disappointment and low self-esteem. The low self-esteem produces an overwhelming sense of guilt, not because we have done anything bad but because we never feel we have 'made the grade'. This begins to affect the way we relate to others, always frightened of doing the wrong thing, trying hard to please and needing to earn acceptance. Every time we think we have done wrong it throws us into self-condemnation and an even greater lack of worth. The self-condemnation and lack of worth are a prison of isolation.

At times do you feel trapped in that prison? The only way out is by recognising the unreality of some emotions. When they arise it's important to replace the wrong thinking behind them, such as 'I always mess things up', with the truth.

We must dismantle negative emotions based on unreality by recognising what lies behind them. We must also learn how to communicate, but not dwell on, negative emotions that can arise from real events. For instance, you may feel angry because someone has been inconsiderate. It is necessary to admit that anger to yourself, and in some situations express this to others. Once you have admitted it, you need to lay it down so that it doesn't dominate your thinking.

If we can't express our feelings and communicate these to others we seriously jeopardise meaningful relationships. If we haven't been used to expressing and communicating then we need to begin to do it with someone we trust. When my PA first came to work with me I used to find it extremely difficult because she would not communicate how she felt. A relationship of trust built up but still she took a long time to come to the point of communicating what she wanted to say. One day I challenged her about the fact that it was unfair on me if she didn't communicate and that I was not there to guess what was going on. Within no time at all she moved from being 'frozen', and unable to communicate, to saying exactly how she felt. Now she is so open we can communicate in seconds! God can and does work miracles in the area of feelings. When you can communicate your feelings to others you feel far less alone.

Truth

Now to him who is able to do immeasurably more than all we ask or imagine, according to his power that is at work within us ... be glory.

(Ephesians 3:20)

Action

1. If your emotions are 'frozen' trust God to deal with you gently and at a pace you can accept. Tell Him what you fear about emotions and ask Him gradually to bring release for you.
2. Start to notice different emotions, but do not dwell on them.
3. Make a commitment to communicate how you feel and to challenge emotions based on unreality.

8 | EMPTINESS

Have you ever spent a long time relating to someone whom you thought was a close friend and yet you came away feeling as if something was missing? You thought the friendship was good, yet you remained empty and something inside you told you there could be more.

Very few people have close friendships where they can laugh and cry, talk and be silent, affirm and correct each other and where even under extreme pressure the friendship grows. A good friend is like a glove that fits perfectly. There are no gaps and the glove is not restricted but moves with the hand. It also keeps the hand warm. The hand is not dependent on it for survival but the two go well together.

When you have such a friendship you don't struggle with loneliness. The friendship is based on a relationship of give and take, where you feel mutually understood and you have mutual respect. You may be different but the differences complement each other. Irritants are like sand in an oyster's shell. The oyster takes the piece of grit and coats it in layer upon layer of a milky substance until a pearl is created. Out of weaknesses grow strengths and through difficulties the friendship deepens.

Although I believe such friendships are God-ordained, they can only happen when the friendship is built on a healthy foundation. I had to wait many years for the kind of friendship which I am talking about. There were plenty of times in my life when I didn't understand why I had never found this kind of friendship. I even felt angry towards God for not meeting my needs and fooled myself into believing that I didn't need anyone. Why did God 'withhold' what would have made such a difference to my state of loneliness? I am sure that in my case it was for two reasons:

1. My total security was not in Him and so the friendship would have been at the expense of my relationship with Him.
2. I had unhealed hurts from my past which interfered with my relating to people; hence the friendship would have consisted of emotional needs rather than healthy relating.

Most people desire close friendships but don't realise that such friendships can't exist if the relating has unhealthy factors. Some of the common factors which interfere in friendships are:

- wanting to be parented or wanting to parent the other person
- trying to change the other person
- being jealous or possessive
- seeing the other person as meeting unmet childhood needs
- being exclusive: not developing any other friends
- not giving the other person any freedom
- fantasising about the person and being unrealistic, especially concerning his or her weaknesses
- not being able to see yourself as separate from the other person, or by trying to be like them
- not being completely open and honest
- not sharing or expressing your feelings

In our pursuit of friendship we need to make sure that the friendship only develops out of a growing inner security. If we look to another person in order to feel better about ourselves we are in danger of losing the friendship.

Friendship must never be a substitute for working through our problems, hurts or feelings of loneliness. True friendship frees us to share our joys and sadness, our strengths and weaknesses. It enriches our life and personality, frees us to be ourselves and doesn't restrict growth but enhances it.

For deep friendships to work there has to be commitment which requires sacrificing an element of our freedom. Many people struggle to get the balance between freedom and commitment and hence they never make deep friendships. What does commitment mean?

- loving unconditionally
- sticking by your friend in the hard times
- laying aside your own needs for your friend's needs
- keeping confidences
- giving of your time, even when you desire space
- being prepared to listen and understand
- sticking up for your friend when he or she is being criticised

Another vital factor in friendship is communication. If we don't communicate how we feel, and understand how our friends feel, then our friendships are in danger of becoming shallow. There's a price to pay for true friendship and it is the giving of ourselves. Sadly, many people do not give of themselves and consequently never taste close friendships.

Giving of ourselves involves:

- being open and honest
- letting the friend know the 'real' you
- desiring what is best for the friend
- readily forgiving
- having a heart for reconciliation
- being an encourager
- being sincere in all you do

- trusting others with your innermost being
- being hurt and being prepared to work through the hurt

We are often frightened of giving of ourselves and trusting others and so 'hold back' a part of ourselves. The more we 'hold back', the more we experience loneliness. For many people the problem is that whilst they want deep friendships they attempt to develop them with the wrong people. In life you will find very few people with whom you can develop the kind of friendship I'm talking about.

We *choose* our friends and need to be careful in our choice. A friend isn't someone who criticises, pulls down, or uses and leaves you out at their own convenience. Such 'friendships' are unhealthy, but we often allow ourselves to remain trapped in them because we're so desperate for close friendship and we keep making excuses for the way the 'friend' treats us. Sometimes this can also be because we lack self-respect. There are two simple rules in friendship:

1. Do not put the other person down.
2. Do not put yourself down.

Close, meaningful friendships have much to do with freedom from loneliness. Although such friendships are rare they are worth seeking until they are found. In order to develop close friendships you must also get rid of any hang-ups you may have regarding the word 'intimate' because it is an intimate friendship which takes away loneliness. People often view intimacy as something only for marriage and think that there is something profoundly wrong with you if you relate the word to same-sex friendships. Intimacy is sharing, being real and open, not hiding any secrets and having a deep platonic love. There is an intimacy in the Trinity – Father, Son and Holy Spirit – and we are made in their image. You are as lonely as your lack of intimacy.

Do you have a friend you can laugh with and cry with, confront and be confronted by, knowing that it will bring positive change? If you don't have someone you can say anything to, spend regular time with, whom you feel completely accepted and at ease, ask God to give you such a person. The God I know is gracious and faithful and meets our needs. But remember that whilst God can bring the person or people along your path, it takes two people working together to create an intimate friendship. You have to work together to maintain a deep friendship, not allowing the struggles to destroy what God has given.

Truth

A man of many companions may come to ruin, but there is a friend who sticks closer than a brother.

(Proverbs 18:24)

Action

1. Spend time reviewing your friendships. Are there any friendships in which you have tried to create closeness, but which, you now realise, will not work?
2. Spend time reviewing your own way of relating and whether you are able to give of yourself in friendships. Ask God to help you.
3. Commit all your friendships to God and ask Him to release you from any which are not causing you to be free from loneliness. Ask Him to show you how to develop healthy intimacy with the right friends.

9 | LEARNING TO COMMUNICATE

We often feel gagged when we struggle to communicate with others. Poor, or indirect, communication makes us feel very alone as we are unable to express ourselves and so we are more easily misunderstood. We also don't experience the rewards of interaction, of knowing exactly where we stand with others and where they stand with us. The most common form of indirect communication is using behaviour rather than words: for instance, storming out of a room is a way of saying 'I'm angry', and putting someone else down is a way of saying 'something's threatening me'. But because there isn't honesty regarding what is really going on, there's a breakdown in relationship and lack of resolution. If you can't say how you feel then the feelings often go on festering for a long time, bubbling under like a volcano.

Healthy verbal communication is the heartbeat of relationships, and we need to develop it. This form of communicating involves being open and honest and saying exactly what the situation is. In this way we're able to avoid many misunderstandings and deal with problems as they arise, which creates more lasting and meaningful relationships. When we communicate effectively each day life becomes richer, because we're acting on a more emotionally mature basis. On the other hand, indirect communication keeps us in a state of childishness, lack of trust, fear of being hurt and consequent loneliness.

If communication makes such a difference to our relationships and has a huge bearing on the state of loneliness, why do people find it so hard to communicate?

1. Because they have never been taught how to communicate.
2. Because they fear that in communicating the other person may react and/or feel badly towards them.

Let's examine both these difficulties:

1. *Because they have never been taught how to communicate.*
Healthy communication is a skill and like most skills the best way of learning is through observation and being taught. But childhood can just as easily teach us poor communication as it can good communication. Unless we are 're-educated' we blindly carry out our indirect communication and suffer the consequences.

When you haven't been taught to communicate openly how do you make the transition? Ideally you need someone who is skilled in this area to disciple you – that is, to 'walk' with you in your everyday life, pointing out when you are not communicating adequately and giving you examples of how to communicate. For instance, suppose someone says something to you that hurts, even though their intention is not to be hurtful. You retreat to your room, curl up in a ball and go over and over what was said. You become withdrawn and don't want to talk when a friend asks you how you are. The way you're reacting is communicating the fact that you are hurt, but because you don't verbalise it you don't resolve it and your altered mood could now last for days.

Now suppose your friend tells you to say what is bothering you and keeps 'pushing' you until you do. You tell her and she encourages you to talk to the person who hurt you, giving you an outline of what to say. You pluck up the courage and do so. The person who hurt you apologises and there is an end to the situation. Although at first you may need prompting and to be shown guidelines, the more you put this direct form of communication into practice the easier it becomes. This then enables you to take charge of situations for yourself.

2. *Because they fear that in communicating the other person may react and/or feel badly towards them.*
Fear of being hurt, misunderstood or rejected are three of the most common reasons behind not wanting to communicate. Open communication takes courage and it means risking being vulnerable. But what we often fail to realise is that lack of communication causes as much, in fact usually far more, pain than communication does. Think of the example I've just given: if you don't communicate when you're hurt you can easily 'go in on yourself' and experience an excruciating inner agony for days. Whilst the courage needed for communicating can seem too much, and your heart can be pounding, with a little 'push' from yourself the agony of the thought of saying what is on your mind can be over in seconds, with no repercussions.

If you want to make a breakthrough in communication you have to make the choice to be committed in this area, and to see the dangers of not communicating. You must also be honest with yourself and with others, otherwise you defeat the object of communication. Successful communication also means letting go of masks and coping mechanisms, and being real. When we communicate we need to say what is on our mind and how we feel. But it needs to be done in love and without judgment, for the purpose of building one another up, not tearing one another down.

When we do have the desire to communicate openly and directly but it doesn't appear to work it's often due to lack of clarity. What we say and how other people interpret our words can be two very different things. We need to learn how to communicate in different ways to suit different people. Some people need simple communication; others need what is said clarified by illustrations and examples.

To communicate we have to learn to express ourselves. For some people that may not come naturally; for others it may be natural but has been 'killed off' through painful experiences. I remember how, for years, if anyone gave me a present I used to be grateful yet unable to say 'thank you' with any meaning. It felt agony to get any words out and instead I would send a card to thank them a few days later. People assumed I was ungrateful and their misunderstanding of me just added to my frozen state of not being able to express myself. In order to resolve this I had to spend time being helped, and asking God for His release in the area of expression. As soon as I was free in this area I noticed how my relationship changed. Why? Because I was expressing myself and so people knew where they stood!

There are various means of communicating other than through words, such as touch and having time for people, although these should not entirely replace words. It is also not merely communication which is vital but *how* one communicates. The following are a few guidelines which provide some understanding of what communication involves:

1. Communicating through words that the other person can easily understand.
2. Not expecting the other person to read your mind.
3. Thinking through and choosing your words carefully before communicating what is on your mind.
4. Making sure you tackle the problem and not the person!
5. Using 'I' statements and not 'you' statements (I feel, rather than you make me feel).
6. Admitting your failings and readily forgiving.

Remember that as you communicate and build healthier relationships with people your loneliness will lessen. Whenever you are fearful of communicating bear in mind the difference it will make, in the long term, to your state of loneliness and deep inner pain. One of the best ways of becoming more able to communicate is to dare to try. We can always grow when we plant a little seed, but if we refuse to plant a seed there can never be growth.

Truth

Pleasant words are a honeycomb, sweet to the soul and healing to the bones.

(Proverbs 16:24)

Action

1. Be honest with yourself and with others.
2. Ask God to give you a strong desire to communicate healthily, and ask Him to give you someone who can 'model' communication for you.
3. Gradually practise communication and notice the difference in how you feel about yourself, and how other people treat you when you do.

10 | FEELING IMPRISONED

I remember asking a teenager I was helping to draw a picture of how she felt. On a number of occasions she had talked of the word 'black' and I thought it would help her to see what her blackness was. She drew a cross section of a pit. On top of the pit was evidence of life: trees, sky, people. A ladder went down into the pit and in the bottom, in a small box, she drew a cross which marked where she was. She was obviously in a personal prison, and it seemed impossible to imagine her out of the box, climbing the ladder into the open.

Despite the fact that there was a real helplessness represented in her picture there was in fact incredible hope! I said to her, 'If your box had a keyhole where would you put the key?'. I expected her to put the key on the outside, as if she was waiting for someone to rescue her. But she did quite the opposite: she placed the key on the inside of the box.

Typically, when we're struggling, we think that someone else has the answer to our hurts and we passively wait to be rescued. This automatically puts us in the position of being a victim. If, on the other hand, we grasp hold of the fact that we already have the answer and it's up to us to put it into operation, we move from a position of powerlessness to a position of strength. We can view our relationship with God in the same way: passively wait for Him to be who He says He is or believe who He is and trust in His promises.

I remember how I used to wait for my loneliness to go and looked to external things to take it away. I felt weak, and angry with people and God; life didn't seem to make sense. Perhaps that's how you're feeling now: longing for someone to change your state of loneliness. Maybe you've not yet grasped the fact that the only person who can change your loneliness is you, by your co-operation with God. If you want to co-operate and recognise that the key is within your reach how do you take hold of the key and unlock the box? Then once you're out of the box how do you get from the bottom of the pit to the top?

The key is in the keyhole; you have already been given it. But you have to choose to use what you've been given. If someone wants to give you a present you don't stand with your arms folded, say thank you and then become frustrated because you can't see what's inside the wrapping paper! You have to open your arms, reach out, take hold of it and undo it. Only then can you truly appreciate what you have been given. In the same way, God has given us fullness of life but we have to take hold of that life to receive our freedom.

When you envisage yourself inside the box at the bottom of the pit of loneliness you must know that your only way out is through Jesus. The means of unlocking the box is by fixing our eyes on Jesus; each rung of the ladder represents accepting what we have been given through Jesus.

Various rungs of the ladder have been, and will be, covered in this book, but there are two I want to focus on in this chapter.

1. God, through Jesus, is our source of life.
2. God offers us mercy.

1. *God, through Jesus, is our source of life.*
Jesus said, 'I am the way and the truth and the life. No-one comes to the Father except through me' (John 14:6). When we give our lives to Jesus we are declaring that He is our source of life, He is the One in whom our needs are met.

People frequently say that Jesus is their source of life and yet at the same time try to make life work on their own. Jeremiah 2:13 says, 'My people have committed two sins: they have forsaken me, the spring of living water, and have dug their own cisterns, broken cisterns that cannot hold water'.

We do not always think about what the broken cisterns (storage tanks) may be and blindly carry on trying to fill them with water whilst all the time they are leaking, and we are remaining empty. If Jesus says, 'Come to me' and we try to find life through acceptance, materialism, marital status, qualifications, etc, then we are not drinking from the spring of living water but rather filling our cisterns with our own water. It's not that what we desire in life is necessarily wrong, but a problem exists if our security is dependent upon these things and we forsake the living water. If we are made for drinking pure water, impure water will never satisfy us. We need, above all else, the pure water God offers us if our thirst is to be quenched.

2. *God offers us mercy.*
God's mercy for us put Jesus on the Cross, to save us from eternal separation from Him. His mercy gives us the water we need to quench our thirst. Those two actions in themselves are too amazing for words, but even more amazing is that His offer is free.

Isaiah 55 begins:

> Come, all you who are thirsty,
> come to the waters;
> and you who have no money,
> come, buy and eat!
> Come, buy wine and milk
> without money and without cost.

Imagine if God had offered us His pure water, which is the

only thing to quench our thirst, and then He had told us that the price was beyond our means! We would feel that we would have to spend our life working to earn enough to purchase what we need. But instead God's offer to us of life and mercy are free gifts. We can't earn God's gifts: they are given. All we must do is receive them.

God's mercy is His compassion, lovingkindness and favour. His act of mercy was not only as a one-off action to save us from eternal separation – His mercies are new every morning!

Because of the Lord's great love
we are not consumed,
for his compassions never fail.
They are new every morning;
great is your faithfulness.

(Lamentations 3:22–23)

Have you ever done something wrong and gone to bed at night with the guilt of what you have done worrying you? You long to start your life afresh without the weight of your actions hanging heavily over you. You would give anything to have the slate wiped clean and be free again. God's offer is, when you come to Him, to wake up in the morning with a brand-new life. He doesn't hold our wrongdoings against us. His compassions never fail, they are new every morning.

If we don't receive His free offer of mercy and if we don't receive Jesus as our source of life we are one rung further down the ladder. We are that bit closer to being imprisoned at the bottom of the pit: with each truth we accept we climb a rung higher.

Are you drinking deep from God's reservoir of love, compassion and kindness. Come, if you have nothing left inside you, come drink and be filled.

Truth

> With God we shall gain the victory...
> (Psalm 60:12)

Action

1. Keep your eyes fixed on Jesus.
2. Ask God to show you what rungs you need to climb next.
3. Spend time thanking God that through Him you will gain the victory over your loneliness.

11 | *VULNERABILITY*

The state of loneliness can leave you feeling raw and vulnerable. When you graze yourself physically you see raw, pink skin which is tender and exposed. If left uncovered it is vulnerable to infection. It hurts when touched and causes you to withdraw. Loneliness is very much the same.

Since loneliness creates such rawness and vulnerability it is dangerous to leave it undealt with. Like any wound, if it is untreated, it becomes messy and is so much harder to clear up. We need healing from our raw and vulnerable state. But where can we find true healing without feeling even more exposed? In Jesus.

1 Peter 2:24 declares about Jesus, '... by his wounds you have been healed'. So it is by Jesus that we receive our healing from hurts; in effect, by applying Him to our wounds. The reason Jesus can make a difference to our wounds is because of the wounds He received. He was marred, defaced and killed so that our hurts could be healed. He did not endure such suffering for us to stay in suffering; He endured beatings, scorn, crucifixion and death that we might be free from our suffering.

Although it's biblical to say that 'by his wounds we are healed', it's unhelpful to most people if they don't know how to relate this to themselves. It leaves people perplexed and angry that they don't experience the healing spoken of. To know our healing through His wounds Jesus must become like an oil to us, poured over and seeping deep into our wounds.

In biblical times oil was used on many occasions and often different spices were added to the oil – myrrh, for instance. Myrrh has several interesting functions. It is both a preservative and a disinfectant and in the same way Jesus preserves our lives and cleanses our wounds. However, myrrh did not preserve or cleanse simply by people looking at it or smelling it, it had to be applied. We need to come to Jesus believing that He wants to bring healing and knowing that He can. As we give Him our hurts imagine seeing Jesus nailed to the cross, carrying our pain. Now imagine that pain dying with Him and as He is raised from the dead, that pain being changed into a healed life. We can begin to thank Him that His love for us replaces other people's hurtful actions towards us.

Myrrh is also used as a painkiller. Don't you long for the pain of loneliness to subside? When Jesus was on the cross He was offered wine mixed with myrrh to drink, but we're told that He did not take it (see Mark 15:23). The myrrh would have deadened some of the pain for Him; He refused it because He knew He had to take the full weight of the pain which enabled Him to identify with every experience we go through in life: the price was paid for all sin and sickness. There is no pain too deep for Jesus to heal.

Finally, myrrh was used as a means of making oneself beautiful. In the Old Testament we read that 'Before a girl's turn came to go in to King Xerxes, she had to complete twelve months of beauty treatments prescribed for the women, six months with oil of myrrh and six with perfume and cosmetics' (Esther 2:12). Jesus makes us beautiful when we allow our lives to become saturated with Him. When we are full of Jesus, and He radiates out of us, a natural beauty shines from the inside out.

If you want beauty to grow out of the rawness of your hurts come into the presence of Jesus. When you hurt do you draw aside and see yourself close to Him? Do you allow His words to be tenderly spoken into your heart and spirit? Do you spend time feeling the warmth of His love surrounding you? One of my favourite ways of doing this is to choose a music tape where the lyrics are based on Scripture and the music is gentle. I then sit or lie and allow the songs to minister to me.

God says to you, in the midst of your wounds:

... I am he who will sustain you. I have made you and I will carry you; I will sustain you and I will rescue you.

(Isaiah 46:4)

I, even I, am he who comforts you.

(Isaiah 51:12)

Spend time allowing these words to sink deep into your spirit and, as you do so, know that each word brings you closer to healing from your raw and vulnerable state.

Truth

... He gathers the lambs in his arms and carries them close to his heart ...

(Isaiah 40:11)

Action

1. Acknowledge Jesus as the One who brings healing and comfort to your raw, vulnerable state.
2. Draw near to Jesus, and allow His presence to saturate you. Spend time with Him feeling His gentleness touching you, preserving your life, cleansing your wounds, numbing your pain, making you beautiful.
3. Jesus longs to gather you in His arms and to carry you close to His heart, where you are warm and safe. Come to Him and let Him pick you up.

12 | HELPLESSNESS

Imagine a vast army approaching you. You feel totally helpless, powerless and you fear for your life.

Spiritually and emotionally it can often feel as if there's a great army about to descend upon us. We're weary of trying to fight when we seem so weak in comparison with the force of what is coming our way. Frequently we feel we're fighting single-handedly; we long for the day when others will come and help, or better still when we won't have to fight at all!

Jehoshaphat, King of Judah, felt exactly the same when his territory was about to be invaded. He was warned that a vast army was approaching and even though he was afraid he sought the Lord. All the people of Judah came together and Jehoshaphat stood before them and prayed. He proclaimed the might and power of God and reaffirmed God's promise that the land would remain theirs. He then declared before God that although he and his people didn't have the power to fight or to know what to do, they would keep their eyes on Him. He had the faith to believe that God would be faithful to them.

> Then the Spirit of the Lord came upon one of the men present and said, 'Listen, King Jehoshaphat and all who live in Judah and Jerusalem! This is what the Lord says to you: "Do not be afraid or discouraged because of this vast army. For the battle is not yours, but God's ..."'
>
> (2 Chronicles 20:15)

The Lord declared that the battle was not theirs but His.

They had to submit to God and be obedient to Him and not fight in their own strength. Many of us have a lesson to learn here: instead of just rushing off and doing our own thing, we need to hear God and act on what He is saying. When we do this we know that we will win.

One of the battles relating to loneliness I tried to fight alone, time and time again in the past, was to do with singleness. No doubt some of you are fighting that very same issue at the moment. You desire marriage and children and watch both the biological clock tick by and friends around you find partners. But where is your partner? There's an inner aching aloneness as you long for a mate and children of your own. You begin to believe that your freedom from loneliness depends upon marriage, and for as long as marriage is not yours you hurt. Not having anyone special, going home to an empty house, and eating Sunday lunch alone simply adds to the pain.

I went through years of inner torment along these lines. God gave me promises about marriage but in my aloneness I just agonised over whether I had 'got it right', and asked why it wasn't happening. Not until I handed the problem over to God and declared the battle His, not mine, did I stop hurting, find fulfilling friendships with both sexes and start to enjoy life! This showed me how important it is to trust God and to hold on to His promises for our lives, even when we don't see any evidence of them. We can learn from the prayer which Jehoshaphat prayed in a battle situation. There were various stages in his praying.

Firstly, Jehoshaphat acknowledged who God is and declared His power and might. When we are facing a difficult situation we too can automatically jump in and start calling out to God. The first commandment is to love God with all our heart and, whatever our circumstances, we need to put Him first and give Him all the praise and honour due to Him.

When we praise God and focus on His holiness, power and authority, without even mentioning our situations, we move from a place of despondency to a place of hope. We begin to see how great God is and so believe He can work in all situations. We start to get things in perspective.

Secondly, Jehoshaphat declared aloud what God had already done. There are two important principles here. One is the declaring aloud before witnesses and the other is acknowledging what God has done for you. It's so easy when facing difficult situations to doubt what God has done and said. This is one of Satan's oldest tricks. In the Garden of Eden he whispered to Eve, 'Did God really say, "You must not eat from any tree in the garden"?' We must hold fast to what God has said, even if circumstances look as if they're going in a completely different direction. Jehoshaphat knew that God had given the land to the descendants of Abraham for ever and that they had built a sanctuary for God.

Thirdly, Jehoshaphat believed God's promise – he was not going to stand back and simply allow the land to be taken over. A righteous anger rose up within him – even if a little fear was mixed with it! When God gives us a promise and things come against us we must not just give up. Instead we must hold on to every word from God. If we have not heard God, we must seek Him until we know what He is saying.

Fourthly, Jehoshaphat admitted that in their own strength they had no power to face the vast army and so declared before God, 'We do not know what to do, but our eyes are upon you'. Admitting our helplessness, seeing God's power and allowing Him to take control, is something which many of us do not find easy. We have all sorts of misconceptions about how we ought to be strong, and how not battling alone is a sign of weakness and lack of faith. We feel it is wrong to ask for help.

Do you feel as though an army is advancing against you sometimes? The 'army' could be people, situations, unresolved hurts, expectations, or unanswered questions. Try not to look at the size of the 'army' and become fearful. Act as Jehoshaphat did, taking various steps to deal with the problem. Make sure you only concentrate on one step at a time and always keep your focus on God.

Truth

Our help is in the name of the Lord, the Maker of heaven and earth.

(Psalm 124:8)

Action

1. Admit that in your own strength you can't fight situations but with God all things are possible.
2. When God gives you a promise, but you don't see change, hold on to the promise and not what appears to be before your eyes.
3. Learn to give thanks and praise to God in all circumstances, remembering what He has done for you.

13 | REALISTIC EXPECTATIONS

Have you ever had expectations of life, yourself, others or even God, and come away feeling let down? We all have! High but particularly unrealistic expectations lead to loneliness, because they result in disappointment.

What are some of the expectations you might have?

1. God should just take away my loneliness.
2. God should bring the right people around me to fill in the emptiness.
3. If God loves me He would not put me through this terrible feeling.
4. Other people should understand how I feel.
5. Other people should ask me how I am.
6. Other people should know what I need.
7. If I am of any worth then I would be included in things by others.

To be free from much of the emotional pain of loneliness we need to have realistic expectations. If we look at some of the above in more detail you'll be able to get a better picture of what I mean by realistic expectations.

1. *God should just take away my loneliness.*
People can become quite angry with God when they ask Him over and over again to do something and there's no result. If loneliness is made up of various things in a person's life, each of which need addressing, and God took away the loneliness would it really help the person? No, not if we still relate in the same way and have the

same expectations of God and others. We need to see change in our relationship with God, our priorities and our interaction with people, to avoid replacing the loneliness with another problem. No longer lonely, but obsessive! When I talk about freedom from loneliness I do *not* think of another problem developing!

Another reason why expecting God simply to take away loneliness is an unrealistic expectation is that we need to know that some aspects of loneliness have personal responsibility. Saying this does not decry God's healing power. God can, of course, do anything but at the same time He is not a magician. I believe that His work in our lives is to a certain extent in the context of relationship with Him.

I remember a period in my life when I'd been physically ill for several years. I cried out to God over and over again to heal me, but nothing happened. At the time there was a lot of spiritual compromise in my life and I wasn't walking with God in the way that I am now. When my relationship with God changed and I put Him first, rejected compromise and put into operation His principles, I could cry out to God for my healing and I found it! It taught me a big lesson about personal responsibility.

2. *God should bring the right people around me to fill in the emptiness.*

Have you ever felt that meaningful friendships would make all the difference to your loneliness? With each person you meet you try to build the kind of friendship you need but something always seem to go wrong or you end up feeling hurt and let down. You don't understand why God is not bringing people along whom you believe would make a difference. Although other people are significant to our not experiencing loneliness, overcoming loneliness has much more to do with our own self-acceptance and emotional maturity. As this develops so also will healthy relating and the ability to know with whom to build friendships.

3. *If God loves me He would not put me through this terrible feeling.*

Our expectations of God can be way off course! Not only do we expect Him to do things for us which are our responsibility but we judge His love for us by how our lives are going! If we are to be free from loneliness (and many others things) we need to have an accurate picture of God, the devil, and personal responsibility. Imagine a house being burgled in the night whilst everyone is asleep, and in the morning the child saying to his mother, 'Why did you let the burglar in? If you loved me he wouldn't have burgled our house'. It sounds crazy, but we do precisely that with God! We need to remember that God loves us despite what is going on in our lives. Therefore what goes on in our lives is not necessarily an indicator of His love for us.

4. *Other people should understand how I feel.*

When we expect others to understand how we feel it can lead to disappointment. When our communicating and relating is not healthy we expect other people to guess how we feel and often wait for someone to say something. We read into actions: 'If someone puts their arm around me it means they care; if they don't put their arm around me it means they don't care', etc. We frequently measure how much people care by whether they show an interest in us, know how we are feeling or know what we need.

It's very healing to have people around who understand us and it's something that we all want, and it may even help us in terms of our security and emotional maturity. However, it must be our responsibility to communicate how we feel and we must accept the limitations of the other person. The other person is also human, with limited understanding and with their own needs and feelings.

I remember fairly early on in leadership realising that, despite having a very close friendship with someone with whom I could freely communicate on all occasions, I could not have too high expectations of this friend. Although I shared everything with her and always felt very understood, there was one day when I was experiencing a deep pain in relation to the weight of leadership and wanting to run from my role. I knew that this was something which only God could understand and that it was to Him alone I must turn. If I had expected my friend to understand, my expectations would have been too high. When my expectations were too high, I would have ended up feeling disappointed.

Envisage standing at the top of a very high mountain looking down. The peak of the mountain represents unrealistic expectations whilst the hard ground below represents the disappointment. When we set unrealistic expectations which consequently lead to disappointment it is very much like bungee jumping from the top of the mountain! People who constantly set high expectations of others experience the ups and downs between the mountain and hard ground below. If we desire stability in our lives we must walk along the middle path halfway up the mountain where there is a healthy balance between other people's care and understanding and being on our own.

Have you learned how to establish the balance in your life between other people caring and understanding and you taking responsibility? Do you know yourself and other people sufficiently to be sure of how high your expectations should be? If not, give some thought to these things and maybe ask other people who have learned this art to show you in practice how to develop it in your life.

Truth

It is better to take refuge in the Lord than to trust in man.

(Psalm 118:8)

Action

1. Ask God, and emotionally mature Christians, to show you whether there are unrealistic expectations, and unhealthy ways of relating, in your life.
2. Repent of blaming God for things which were your responsibility or the devil's doing.
3. Commit each area to God and ask for His help.

14 | DEALING WITH JEALOUSY

We don't like to see ourselves as jealous people and yet it is jealousy we're harbouring when we look at others and think that their grass is greener than ours. I expect there have been occasions when you have come away from spending time with people and felt very alone because you are comparing your life with theirs. The empty holes in your life seem to be emphasised when you apparently see them being filled in someone else's life.

There are a couple of things I have learned over the years in relation to feeling that the grass is greener where someone else is:

1. Grass from a distance can look greener than it really is.
2. Grass which is not very green needs watering.

Let's look at both these observations.

1. *Grass from a distance can look greener than it really is.*
The grass which others are standing on may not be as green as you perceive it to be. We often see other people's grass as very green for two reasons a) because we fail to see their life as a whole or b) because we're comparing our lives with theirs. Let me explain in more detail what I mean by these.

When we look at other people it's often through the lenses of jealousy. We mainly look at what other people have that we don't have. Rarely do we look at what we have that they don't have! It's true that other people have what we desire but it's also true that they have deficiencies and 'holes' in their lives. I remember a number of years ago how I frequently saw a friend's grass as far greener than mine. She was only a few years older and had a nice home, a car, a husband and three lovely children. I, on the other hand, was single, living in a shared house and getting from A to B on a push bike. My grass was distinctly brown in my eyes! The ironic thing was that she envied my freedom and ability to do what I chose with my spare time. She also envied my career and the fact that in her eyes I had my whole life ahead of me.

We compare our grass with someone else's grass and label the other person's green, when in fact they are both green. Deep green and pale green are still green! We can badly want what others have and yet if we had it we wouldn't be happy because it's not God's vision for us. Have you ever seen an outfit on someone else and desired it? When you try it on it looks awful and you then realise that it wasn't made for you but for the other person. Rather than comparing our life with others we need to have a strong vision for our own life. A vision for our life is like a magnet which pulls us out of a state of loneliness and actually fills our lives. I don't believe that we know fulfilment until we know, and are operating in, God's plan for our lives.

2. *Grass which is not very green needs watering.*
Sometimes, when someone else's grass looks greener it's due to our grass being dry. In this case what's needed is to give our grass more moisture and feeding. Is your grass the greenest it can be at the moment? If we don't water and feed plants they wither, and if continually not watered they die. If we don't water and feed our spirit it will become lifeless. Just as a plant needs to be watered to flourish, and a muscle needs working to develop, so your spirit needs to be fed and exercised in order to grow. Mature Christians are eating and exercising spiritually all

the time! What nourishment does your spirit need to be rich in colour? It needs to:

- praise and worship God every day
- have fellowship with Jesus
- be continually filled with the Holy Spirit
- feast on the word of God
- receive regular revelation
- walk in love and forgiveness towards everyone
- have faith even in the most difficult moments
- listen to God regularly
- be encouraged and corrected by fellow believers
- pray for others using the gifts of the Holy Spirit

Are you allowing your spirit to be fed regularly? Feeding is essential and it's mainly for this reason that people go to Christian conferences and buy Christian books and tapes. Some churches do not feed their sheep sufficiently and so the sheep wander off to other places looking for more nourishing food.

I remember the minister of one church, which was accused of stealing the sheep from other churches, saying that the sheep were hungry and slipped through the fence in search of food! They came to his church for feeding but when they tried to return to their church they were too fat to fit back through the fence! We must not merely be well fed, we must exercise. Exercise involves putting into practice what we are taught, and using the gifts God has given us. Sometimes exercise can feel like hard work because we have to use muscles we don't normally use; we have to be stretched. Only when we are well fed and taking good exercise will our grass become a rich green.

When our grass has a richness to it which only God can give, others too desire that richness. There is a difference between being jealous of what others have, and so being angry or self-pitying that we don't have the same, and being in awe of what others have and desiring to change for the good.

How realistic are you being concerning the grass which others are standing on? Can you see that their grass is not greener but different? Can you see too that if your grass is somewhat dry it will remain like that unless it's watered, nourished and put to good use? We mustn't compare ourselves with others but seek God's will for ourselves as individuals.

Truth

...I am the Lord your God, who teaches you what is best for you, who directs you in the way you should go.

(Isaiah 48:17)

Action

1. If you're jealous of what other people have, ask God what is missing in your life.
2. Find some 'mature' Christians you can spend time with to bring you to that place of desiring change.
3. Look at whether you are in need of greater teaching through conferences or books and tapes, etc.

15 | THAT CONSUMING FEELING

No doubt you've had times when you've felt that your loneliness has consumed you. When you think of the word 'consumed' you think of something which takes over and dominates your time and energy. Being consumed by something negative feels frightening and oppressive. When loneliness consumes it can be like a heavy blanket which is thrown over you and which stays with you wherever you go. Just as you see the light and start to move forward it's as though the fog descends in the most dense and dark form you have known, and your vision is blurred. How do you get out of such a situation?

Firstly, do you want to get out? One of the questions Jesus asked many people before healing them was, 'Do you want to be well?' By asking that He was showing that He knew that there were some people who didn't want to be well, or who were half-hearted about overcoming their problems. Jesus knew that people's desire and faith played an important part in their overcoming. No doubt He also knew that the reason people were half-hearted in wanting to get better was because it was easier to stay as they were; the way of life was familiar, or the patterns were needed as part of their identity and security.

Has loneliness become a familiar way for you, forming part of your identity and security? Have you decided that whatever benefits it had in the past you no longer want these as a part of your life?

Secondly, assuming you do want to get out, where is your focus? Is it on the loneliness or on the path to freedom? When we go through an experience such as loneliness, the pain and fear pull us in the direction of looking at that experience. We soon become preoccupied with our state, and loneliness overwhelms us. When people try to take our attention away from the loneliness we can see it as them misunderstanding how much pain we are going through. The feeling of being misunderstood then keeps us in the position of being preoccupied with loneliness.

Whatever we are consumed by governs our life, attitudes, feelings and even our actions. It's not that being consumed is wrong, but what we are consumed by.

Often when we've been hurt or let down we become consumed by our hurts and needs and so focus on ourselves. We long, somehow, to make up for the deprivation we've experienced, but each effort either makes us feel worse or want more. The way in which most people go about making up for deprivation is by focusing on what they don't have, and longing for someone to meet the need. This merely leads to disappointment and so a further focus on deprivation. For instance, if you're consumed by the need for affection you constantly think about, long for and look for affection. Other people see you as, perhaps, attention seeking and draw back from you. This only creates a deeper need within you. If, instead, you allow yourself to be consumed by the Holy Spirit your focus will be on Jesus and all that you say and do will reflect Him. This in turn will cause other people to see Jesus in you. When we focus on Jesus He becomes more evident in our lives than the loneliness. As we become consumed by Him the loneliness begins to sink into the background, and in time it fades away.

How do you begin to focus on Jesus when the loneliness seems so overwhelming? You have to:

1. Choose to lay the loneliness aside.
2. Choose to believe that spending time with Jesus will make a difference.

3. Choose which way you will find it easiest to enter into Jesus' presence.

1. *Choose to lay the loneliness aside.*

Choosing to lay something aside which we have believed has total control over us isn't easy. You may even be thinking that it sounds impossible. This is because when many people tell us to lay something aside they do so with the underlying message of 'snap out of it'. I know that you can't just snap out of your loneliness, but I also know that you can make a rational decision to remove it from the centre of your life. A good place to begin is to tell God that you are laying your loneliness to one side, and actually hold a picture of moving it in your mind.

To remove loneliness from the centre means making space for other things to come in, giving it less time in our thinking, conversations and even in the way we relate to people.

When we are consumed by loneliness and have not laid it aside we act lonely. We may not be conscious of doing so but other people can often see that we are. Laying aside loneliness can begin as we choose to put into operation the opposite of what we have been doing in many areas, as we move from:

- being entertained to offering hospitality
- saying how we feel to asking how others feel
- looking for friendship to making friendship
- wanting affirmation to giving affirmation
- feeling left out to including those who are left out
- looking for love to giving love
- waiting to be asked to asking

It's amazing the difference it makes to begin to do the opposite of what we've being doing: we get different reactions and results. This is because we have a different attitude towards ourselves, other people and life. We gain a positive and outward-looking approach. This leaves more room for something other than loneliness to be actually at the centre: if more of us is outside ourselves, more of Jesus can be at the centre of us.

2. *Choose to believe that spending time with Jesus will make a difference.*
If we've not convinced that spending time with Jesus will make a difference to our lives then we won't benefit when we do so.

Laying aside our loneliness and then not believing that being in Jesus' presence will fill the centre of our lives means negative things become the centre. Loneliness can so easily be replaced by compulsions and addictions.

Do you believe that spending time with Jesus is going to make a difference? If you do, then whatever means you find yourself using in order to spend time with Him, will draw you into a depth of relationship which brings satisfaction.

3. *Choose which way you will find it easiest to enter into Jesus' presence.*
If you've made the choice to believe that coming into Jesus' presence will make a difference to you then you need to find the easiest way for you to draw close to Him. If you'd decided to climb Mount Everest you wouldn't choose to take the hardest route. Instead you'd find yourself a guide and take it one step at a time, along the most comfortable route to the summit.

There are different means of drawing close to Jesus at different stages in our lives, or even on different days. We get to know what works for us. You may prefer:

- listening to a praise or worship tape
- reading the words of songs as prayers
- singing or playing an instrument
- reading the Bible
- listening to a teaching tape

- imagining yourself standing at God's throne
- feeling yourself like a young lamb secure in the arms of Jesus
- speaking a psalm aloud
- dancing and praising God
- talking to Jesus like a friend

The *means* by which we come into the presence of Jesus are not as important as actually *coming* into his presence. We can do any one of the above out of duty or religiosity; or any one of them can bring us so close to Jesus that we can feel His arms around us.

Knowing that you're wrapped in the loving embrace of Jesus is to be consumed by His love. It's such a precious experience that nothing else compares. The more frequently and longer we're there, the less we want to, or even can, return to the patterns which lie behind our loneliness.

If you don't know what it is to come into the presence of Jesus, ask Him to draw you close to Him as you choose to lay aside your loneliness. Make a conscious decision to spend time with him, and decide how you are going to do this.

Truth

May the God of hope fill you with all joy and peace as you trust in Him, so that you may overflow with hope by the power of the Holy Spirit.

(Romans 15:13)

Action

1. Ask yourself whether you want to be free from loneliness sufficiently to put into action a change of focus.
2. Lay aside your loneliness and believe that coming into the presence of Jesus will make a significant difference to your life.

3. Each day choose a means of coming into the presence of Jesus. Begin to learn the difference between doing these in response to duty and as an act of love.

16 | STOP PRETENDING

Have you ever felt so desperate with loneliness that you'd try anything and everything to be free from it? You try telling people how you feel and end up a moaning, self-pitying and helpless person. Sometimes other people even tell you that you are! Then you decide, 'Whatever happens I won't tell anyone how I feel; I will give the impression that everything is fine'. You move into a world of pretence, only to find that such a state reinforces your loneliness.

I remember writing a poem called 'Pretence' when I was a teenager, the first verse of which read:

> Pretend you're happy when you're blue
> It isn't very hard to do,
> Close your eyes and you'll be there
> To find a world that'll really care.

The temptation to live in a world of pretence is very great, only many people don't even realise that this is what they do. Pretence can take many forms, some of which are more obvious than others but all of which involve not being real. Some of the more obvious forms of pretence include:

- living in a fantasy world
- putting on a façade
- acting out an image
- deception or lying

Less obvious forms of pretence include:

- not letting people get to know all of you
- portraying something which isn't really you inside
- wearing a mask so that people have a different impression of you
- not being open and honest

Not being real creates loneliness and so if we want to be free we must choose to be real. Why does it create loneliness? Because other people don't connect with what is essentially you. Imagine you're at a fancy dress party and someone whom you have wanted to know for a long time, but who isn't in fancy dress, comes up to you. The person begins to talk to you as the character you are portraying. There's no connection with the real you and if the person continues to relate to you as this character (because that is what you are portraying) the lonelier you actually feel.

Being real is essentially being honest, showing all sides of ourselves and not pretending to be someone we're not. When we are being real we:

- having nothing to hide
- show our strengths and weaknesses
- do not try to impress
- share our feelings openly
- give people confidence in knowing where they stand with us
- say what we mean
- are honest with ourself and others

Being real enables us to relax with people because we aren't constantly worried about what they may see, think or find out. Not being real puts us 'on edge' and exhausts us; it's like taking part in a play which has no ending. We may be applauded for our performance but we know that it was only acting.

If being real is so good for us why do we hold back from it and allow pretence to take over? I believe it's because we are frightened of what others may think of us; we need to be approved of; we feel we can't trust others; we feel the need to protect ourselves; or we've been brought up in a world of pretence and haven't had a role model.

We won't be free from pretence until we see that it does more damage than good. If pretence exists to protect us what if someone doesn't like the façade we put up? Their reaction towards us still hurts even if it's a reaction to an outer image. We've nothing to lose by being real. If people affirm us and we have a façade, they are affirming our facade; the real person remains unaffirmed and unconnected. Our pretence may be a comfort zone, but is it better to be safe and lonely or not lonely but vulnerable, knowing that with God's help we can deal with the hurts arising out of our vulnerability?

We need to reach a place where we see our pretence not as a means of protection but as a form of restraint; it restrains us from receiving what will set us free.

If you can now see that you have not been real and that this has been contributing to your loneliness and you desire to be real, make a commitment to follow this route. Ask God to help you to learn, and to put into operation, what being real means. Go back over this chapter highlighting what is currently missing in your life and make a note of the areas which need to change. Can you think of a person who is real to whom you could talk, and ask for their help? If you start to be real you will find that a new world opens up to you and that in the centre of that world is an intimacy you would not previously have known. There is no loneliness in true intimacy.

Truth

Surely you desire truth in the inner parts; you teach me wisdom in the inmost place.

(Psalm 51:6)

Action

1. Ask God to show you what your forms of pretence are.
2. Ask God to give you the courage to let go of pretence and all your masks that go with it.
3. Keep reminding yourself that it's better to be vulnerable and free from loneliness than safe and in a state of loneliness.

17 | BOUND BY THE PAST

Do you think of yourself as bound? The word 'bound' sounds quite dramatic and when you hear the words 'bound by the past' you tend to think of someone in a very bad emotional state. In fact, the dictionary definition of bound is 'limited; restricted'. When our everyday lives, emotions, relationships and freedom from loneliness are limited or restricted by past hurts we are basically 'bound by the past'. Until we're free from the past we're unlikely to be free from loneliness.

If we want freedom from loneliness we must be prepared to face our hurts and patterns of behaviour which still restrict us in so many different ways. We will not be free from these until we believe that it's possible. In the New Testament Paul declared about Jesus, 'It is for freedom that Christ has set us free. Stand firm then and do not let yourselves be burdened again by a yoke of slavery' (Galatians 5:1). It is by Jesus' power that we are set free and through that freedom we can enter into experiences not possible whilst still bound.

Undealt-with past hurts and patterns of behaviour which arise out of those hurts subtly interfere with life. Imagine a group of people all doing a cross-country run. All have been trained, know the route and have about the same ability. Then imagine one of the runners being dressed in heavy boots, ski clothes and with a rucksack full of bricks on his back. Every few minutes he has to stop and frequently he falls over. He is unable to see that what he is wearing has anything to do with why he so easily gives up. With all the others racing on ahead, he feels more and more alone as he is left behind. Each of the bulky items of clothing represents the hurts and patterns from which we need to be healed and set free.

As adults we are often controlled by our childhood. Someone says something to us and we feel or react in a certain way. It's as though all the experiences and wounds from the past sit inside and screen our current experiences. Present situations touch alert buttons and we 'flip' into a different mode. Being free from the past means being free from a wounded child inside screaming 'help' every time a present situation reminds him/her of old feelings. It also means there won't be that sudden change of behaviour. If hurts aren't healed we can end up feeling as though we are two people: one who is acceptable and one who must be hidden. The hidden self is demanding, hurting and wants needs met now, which can leave us feeling ashamed. Often what we try to do is kill this part of ourselves, whilst other people tell us we must repent of it. The hurt part of us needs to be fed with God's truth and to be healed, whilst our behaviour arising out of the hurt needs to be repented of.

Our undealt-with hurts are like a tape recorder which when we relate to others switches itself on. At times we can't hear what others say, only what the tape recorder plays. We turn down the volume so as not to hear but in fact the tape recorder is still playing and directing the way we respond. Maybe you were brought up in a family of tensions and unspoken conflict and now, as an adult, each time there is conflict you feel as isolated, bad and tense as when you were little. The hurts have not been healed and nor have you been taught that people can have different opinions and yet still care for each other.

Are you controlled by the echo of your childhood? Can you see the effect it is having on you? If you desire to be set free then begin to ask God to help you towards freedom. Freedom does not come about through following a formula, but there are several guidelines which can help you to start shedding all the extra baggage you have been carrying, which has weighed you down and restricted you.

How do you know when past hurts are unhealed and continue to affect you? Some, or all of the following may be present:

1. You frequently feel isolated or different.
2. You fear being abandoned.
3. You feel like an orphan.
4. You are unable or too frightened to express certain emotions.
5. You believe others can rescue you.
6. You feel emotionally younger than you are.
7. What other people think of you controls what you do.
8. You fear responsibility and adult life.
9. You think a lot about the past.
10. You are constantly falling out with people or feel misunderstood by them.

After you have asked God to help you, you need to do various things:

1. Bring before God all the situations and people from your past and present life which still hurt you or dominate your thinking. Commit each one to Him. This is important because not only in doing this are you giving God the right to work in these situations, but you are 'owning' them. Whilst you deny they exist or deny their impact, healing cannot take place. There may be more deeply buried hurts but don't go trying to find out what they are. Instead ask God to show you when you are ready to cope with them and willing to hand them over to Him.

2. Ask God to show you all the wrong patterns of behaviour and relating which have arisen as a result of the

hurts. Repent of these and ask God to forgive you.

3. Recognise that many of the hurts and patterns of behaviour have developed out of wounds encountered in childhood. These may have become a part of yourself which you keep hidden, or label 'bad'. Choose to no longer hide or to label them 'bad'. Instead see them as a part of yourself which you have kept locked in a childish state. By acknowledging them and giving them over to God you allow that part of yourself to mature into adulthood.

4. Forgive all the people who have wounded you and also forgive yourself.

5. Don't dwell on your hurts. We must only look at our hurts long enough to acknowledge what they are and to bring them to God. We can't go back into the past, nor can we ever make up for hurts and losses experienced, but God can bring such a deep healing that whilst we remember our past we are no longer affected by it.

God longs to see you whole. When you have been hurt it can be difficult to believe that you can ever be whole. But you can! You have to hold on to the fact that God who created heaven and earth, and who made every snowflake different, has the power to heal every hurt. Nothing is too difficult for Him. We can feel dry and barren, but God will make the rivers flow in the parched land.

> The poor and needy search for water,
> but there is none;
> their tongues are parched with thirst.
> But I the Lord will answer them;
> I, the God of Israel, will not forsake them.
> I will make rivers flow on barren heights,
> and springs within the valleys.
> I will turn the desert into pools of water,

and the parched ground into springs.

(Isaiah 41:17–18)

God *will* heal. He cares for *you*.

Truth

Forget the former things; do not dwell on the past. See, I am doing a new thing!

(Isaiah 43:18–19)

Action

1. Be honest with God about your hurts and your behaviour.
2. Believe that God not only wants to bring healing but will bring healing to you.
3. Submit your hurts to God.

18 | LIFE'S SO UNFAIR

When we've been hurt and we desire change but nothing seems to happen, life can seem very unfair. When life seems unfair it's very easy to start to feel sorry for ourselves, and comparing our life with others just seems to highlight how unfair our life is! But do we allow ourselves to be pulled into the pit of self-pity? For that is exactly what self-pity is: self in a pit where the sides are so slippery that every attempt to come up to the top causes us to slip back down.

This doesn't mean that we won't go through difficult times when we feel sad, but we need to know that there is a difference between a healthy sadness and self-pity. We may feel sad that we don't have something we long for or that something very dear to us has gone. It's not wrong to admit to emotion but if we let that emotion dictate to us we move to the brink of self-pity: e.g. 'my situation is so terrible that no one could understand'.

Self-pity is very unattractive; people are easily put off and draw back from us when we feel sorry for ourselves. It causes us to change into a combination of demanding and rejecting. Maybe without even opening our mouths we demand that others should feel sorry for us and help us; with the same breath we reject them because they could not possibly understand and help in any way! Where does that leave us? Alone. So alone we feel sorry for ourselves.

In Psalm 73 we read of how self-pity became entangled with a bitter and despairing search for a 'trouble-free' life. The psalmist felt that life was unfair because the wicked seemed to have so much more; they were carefree and their wealth increased. He said, 'They have no struggles; their bodies are healthy and strong. They are free from the burdens common to man; they are not plagued by human ills' (Psalm 73:4–5). Don't we often envy people for the same reasons? They have wealth, they don't struggle like we do, and they don't have the same burdens. Fortunately for the psalmist, his envy resulted in confession followed by a declaration of the goodness of God.

Self-pity so often grows out of envy, and the psalmist in this case was no exception. He has kept himself pure and yet he was suffering. 'Surely in vain have I kept my heart pure; in vain have I washed my hands in innocence. All day long I have been plagued; I have been punished every morning' (Psalm 73:13–14). Many of us have used the same plea for justice – 'It isn't fair. I have been obedient and yet things don't work out whilst this person has been continually deceitful and has everything', etc.

Finally the truth dawns and the psalmist turns from self-pity and self-interest to remembering basic responsibilities and loyalties. Although at this stage he didn't have an answer, the shift in attention was a start. Then his eyes are opened and he turns to God in repentance and acknowledgment of all that God is to him: '... you hold me by my right hand. You guide me with your counsel ... But as for me, it is good to be near God. I have made the Sovereign Lord my refuge; I will tell of all your deeds' (Psalm 73:23–24, 28).

The psalmist made a vital shift in focus from feeling sorry for himself to looking to God for an answer. We need to do exactly that with every thought which is heading towards the pit of self-focus. This means starting to correct our thinking. The way we perceive things has a strong bearing on our emotions. If we think negatively we feel negative. For instance, if we say that people don't care about us we will feel down. If we believe they care in their own way and that God loves us, our outlook will be different.

Unless we correct our thinking life will appear more unfair than it actually is. What do you label as unfair? I suggest you write these down and opposite each write the beginning of the answer, based on your eyes being focused on God not yourself. For instance:

Unfair	*Focusing on God*
Other people don't struggle as I do.	God is mighty and will help me to overcome my struggles.
Other people don't trust God and yet things work out for them, but not for me.	God loves me and has a plan and purpose; His love is not dependent upon how well my life is going.

In many respects life is not fair, but whether it is fair or not we still have to hold on to the fact that God is just. Often when we face situations in life which seem unfair we actually feel angry towards God. We somehow see Him as an insurance policy: He is there to prevent us from any hardships in life. We can end up with a trust in God which goes up and down according to how well our lives are going.

Rather than seeing life as unfair we need to see the 'unfair' situations as make or break experiences. We have to decide at the beginning that life's trials are all going to be 'make' experiences. How do they become 'make' experiences? By allowing the grace of God to flow in and through our lives. The New Testament Greek word for grace is 'charis' which means joy, favour, acceptance. It's a favour done without expectation of anything in return and it expresses the absolute lovingkindness of God to a people who don't deserve this.

Sometimes it can seem as though God takes away the good things in our lives, and when we are not allowing the grace of God to flow in our lives we feel that life/God is unfair. But think back to Jesus' death, resurrection and then Pentecost. The disciples must have felt that Jesus had been taken from them and how could anything good come out of His death? But then came Pentecost and they received the Holy Spirit. When Jesus was with them they didn't have His power wherever they went but when the Holy Spirit came He was with them all the time. He said, 'it is better that I go', but not until after Pentecost could they understand exactly what He meant by the word 'better'.

When you next face the feeling that life or a situation is unfair, begin to focus on God's overall plan for your life. Just as something wonderful came out of Jesus' death, your struggles, too, can lead to meaningful events. When you are making a tapestry you often have to check the back for knots or snags. Just because the back may be in a mess doesn't mean that a wonderful picture can't be produced. Keep your eyes fixed on the front!

Truth

> ... he who began a good work in you will carry it on to completion until the day of Christ Jesus.
>
> (Philippians 1:6)

Action

1. Confess before God the times when you have felt He has been unjust to you.
2. Begin to turn some of your 'break' experiences into 'make' experiences.
3. Ask God to help you change your perspective so that life doesn't always appear unfair.

19 | *ANGER*

One of the easiest traps to fall into when we are feeling let down by God and others is the anger and bitterness trap.

What might you be feeling angry about? Perhaps you feel that:

- things never change
- no one seems to care
- everyone has someone else who is a priority
- other people get chosen and you always get left out
- everything is geared towards couples
- God doesn't rescue you
- people keep pointing you towards spiritual change
- other people don't seem to be lonely
- people don't have enough time
- occasions like Christmas and birthdays always result in disappointment

We all, at times, come up against situations which we feel very angry about but there's a big difference between righteous and unrighteous anger. Righteous anger is in response to a situation of injustice. Unrighteous anger is an explosion of emotion, expressed or unexpressed, growing out of wrong expectations, self-pity or unrealistic demands.

Unrighteous anger is also very subtle because we believe we are justified in the way we feel. We are more conscious of feeling that we've had a 'raw deal' in life than we are of the fact that this feeling leads to bitterness.

Ephesians 4:31 says, 'Get rid of all bitterness, rage and

anger, brawling and slander, along with every form of malice'. If we are not careful we can become bitter about people's supposed lack of understanding and sensitivity to our state of loneliness. This can lead to unforgiveness and bitterness about the hurt which arises out of their lack of sensitivity. Bitterness grows into unforgiveness, and the two become like a poison which quickly flows around our bloodstream causing havoc to our system. They result in mistrust and can easily lead to depression. They are also responsible for a lingering sense of grief.

The route of bitterness and unforgiveness is not God's way. He knows how easily we can go from being bitter about one situation to another and then another. God's route is tender-heartedness and forgiveness. Ephesians 4:32 tells us to 'Be kind and compassionate to one another; forgiving each other, just as in Christ God forgave you'.

Forgiveness is one of the main emphases of Jesus' teaching. His words are straight to the point!

> For if you forgive men when they sin against you, your heavenly Father will also forgive you. But if you do not forgive men their sins, your Father will not forgive your sins.
>
> (Matthew 6:14–15)

> Therefore, if you are offering your gift at the altar and there remember that your brother has something against you, leave your gift there in front of the altar. First go and be reconciled to your brother; then come and offer your gift.
>
> (Matthew 5:23–24)

These two passages alone show us the essentials of forgiveness.

1. *Jesus makes it clear that if we forgive, we too are forgiven by God.*

The reason we are to forgive others and show them mercy is because God has forgiven us and shown us mercy, by making a way for us to come back to him and receive eternal life. If we don't forgive it blocks our spiritual growth because we are not in a right relationship with God and consequently not in a right relationship with others. We also block our emotional growth because we remain hooked to the person we are not forgiving and engrossed in the past.

2. *Our gifts or sacrifices are unacceptable to God if, first, we have not forgiven.*

With regards to loneliness this means that if we lay down aspects of our loneliness and honestly desire change it can't be dealt with if we haven't been forgiving. I believe that unforgiveness is one of the main reasons people fail to see change in their lives; because they have not been taught the necessity of forgiving, they don't realise the extent to which it hinders freedom and healing.

Our gifts or sacrifices are also unacceptable without repentance. Repentance involves seeing our wrongs for what they really are, being deeply sorry and turning away from them for good.

If repentance and forgiveness are so essential to freedom why do most people find it so hard to forgive? Perhaps one of the reasons is because we have to humble ourselves. Holding on to bitterness and unforgiveness is a way of holding down the person who has hurt us. We fear that if we let go of our unforgiveness the person may rise up and wound us yet again. We justify our unforgiveness by saying that the other person doesn't deserve to be forgiven. For as long as we are holding on to unforgiveness we feel that the other person is receiving the punishment he or she deserves. But God's teaching is that even if a person wrongs us vengeance is not ours, but God's. We have no right not to forgive because our own lives are not perfect. How can we judge another person's wrongs when we too carry out wrong actions? We just release the person to God; He will deal with them with far more wisdom than we ever could.

Remember, don't wait until you feel like forgiving or you will wait for ever! We need to make a decision of the will because if we don't then we leave an entry point open for Satan. When we put forgiveness and repentance into operation we will see how powerful and liberating they are. They bring restoration and healing. We can't change the past but we have a choice as to how we handle our hurts. By forgiving we not only free ourselves, but we also free the one we are forgiving, from a state of bondage. Are you going to live in the bondage of bitterness or take a big step and choose freedom in forgiveness?

Truth

See to it that no one misses the grace of God and that no bitter root grows up to cause trouble and defile many.
(Hebrews 12:15)

Action

1. Come before God in repentance for any bitterness, unrighteous anger and self-pity you have harboured.
2. Ask God to show you who you need to forgive (do not forget yourself and God!) and make a conscious decision to choose to forgive.
3. Receive God's cleansing and forgiveness for your life too.

20 | No one Understands Me

Why does being misunderstood feel so terrible and create such a cavern of loneliness? I believe it's because you feel as if you have no defence. Often people will go from one misunderstanding to the next, building up a completely wrong picture of you. However hard you try to correct the misunderstanding it can feel as though you simply do not progress in clearing it. You end up feeling powerless, and powerlessness is a feeling that none of us likes.

Being misunderstood is like standing in front of the distorting mirrors you find at fairgrounds. Have you ever been in the maze of mirrors and seen your body change from what it is to being elongated, square or legless? Suppose someone only saw your mirror image and described you according to that. You would want to scream back at them, 'That is not what I am really like; *this* is the real me'. But they can't see what the real you is like because they hold in their mind the distorted image they have.

This can become even more powerful when one misunderstanding leads to another. Imagine the distorted image being held in front of a different mirror altering its image in yet another way. You end up with something far removed from the real you.

This situation was one that happened to me. A couple of people misunderstood me and even with my attempts to explain, it made no difference. It was as though a picture had been drawn up of me which was inaccurate but which others believed and it grieved me deeply. A few months later another incident happened with someone known to those who had misunderstood me which only reinforced the original misunderstanding. This time I wasn't even given the chance to speak for myself. The situation caused me so much pain that I cried out to God for understanding and justice. He said I didn't need to defend myself but that in time people would see the truth.

Suppose I had taken the mirror image that these people had of me and waved it in front of them, saying they had got it all wrong. Their eyes would have been even more focused on the distortion. No! I had to wait until they lifted their eyes from the image and saw the 'real' me.

I waited a year, still subject to deep misunderstanding, before people's eyes were opened and the way I was being viewed changed. Just at this point someone had a word from God for me: 'You have been misunderstood, not by just one person but by several people. These people thought that they were talking about facts relating to you but the facts were wrong and so they were gossiping. The words spoken about you were to pull you down and destroy you. This shall be no more'. The person who received this word from God broke the power of those words over me.

There are so many different ways in which we can feel misunderstood. Some of these *relate* to loneliness and others *create* loneliness. We need to begin to recognise what these may involve so that we can see misunderstanding for what it really is. We need to begin to recognise what these may involve so that we can see misunderstanding for what it really is. Let's look at both types of misunderstanding.

The misunderstandings that *relate* to loneliness are:

1. You are somebody who doesn't care about other people.
2. You are a loner and don't want to make friends.
3. If you suffer from loneliness you are mentally unstable or there must be something wrong with you.

4. You have no desire to be free from loneliness.
5. Loneliness is a sin and all you have to do is repent.
6. Because you have not repented you are in rebellion.

The misunderstandings that *cause* loneliness are:

1. You are said to have done something wrong that you didn't do.
2. You are viewed in a way which isn't accurate or has been taken out of context.
3. Your efforts to make friends are misinterpreted.

There are many misunderstandings which result in a deepening sense of loneliness. You experience loneliness because you feel alone and as if no one understands. Misunderstanding is inevitable but its effects do not have to be. In dealing with misunderstandings we have to remember that revenge and constantly pushing to justify oneself are not the answer. If other people misunderstand us and what they say isn't true, time will prove them wrong.

What then do we do in response to misunderstandings?

1. *Acknowledge to ourselves that we feel misunderstood.*
Sometimes the pain we feel when misunderstood cuts us so deeply that the split second after we have been misunderstood we want to deny it in order to ease the hurt. The other extreme we are sometimes tempted towards is to talk endlessly to others about the injustice of our experiences. Neither of these reactions is helpful and in fact they only cause deeper loneliness. We need to admit to ourselves that we've been misunderstood and begin to see how this may have arisen out of the other person's distorted view of us.

2. *Commit the misunderstanding to God.*
God is the one person who *does* know the truth and who

will not misunderstand you. When we commit things to God we are placing them in His hands so that He can work in the situation. He can more easily open the eyes of the other person to see reality than we can!

When you commit the situation to Him don't only ask that He will bring justice but ask Him to show you if you are wrong in any way. Sometimes a misunderstanding from others can be made worse by our misinterpreting what the other person said. At other times there is truth in what is said but because we can't face the truth we dismiss it and label it as a misunderstanding.

3. *As far as possible correct the misunderstanding.*
It's not right to constantly push to justify oneself but where there is a simple misunderstanding the situation can be cleared up by a word or two. Presenting people with the correct facts is different from demanding that they understand your viewpoint. Where the misunderstanding is more deeply ingrained you can still make an effort to correct it, merely by your actions. Actions speak far louder than words. Letting time heal and also not putting the other person in an uncomfortable position is important.

4. *Pray for the person who misunderstood you.*
Misunderstanding usually happens when we are at our most vulnerable and so feel exposed; making the other person feel exposed is not the answer. We need to pray that what has previously blinded the other person from seeing the truth will be removed. Bless the person and pray for the right opportunity for reconciliation.

Truth

> Be still and know that I am God.
> (Psalm 46:10)

Action

1. If you are currently feeling misunderstood examine your heart to see if there is any truth in the misunderstanding. If there is then ask God's forgiveness.
2. If the misunderstanding is basically not true about you then don't try to justify yourself or take revenge but commit it to God.
3. Ask God to give you a heart to pray for those who persecute you.

21 | UNMET NEEDS

Do your needs ever drive you to the point where you feel that it's your right to have those needs met? At times they do for most of us, but how and where those needs are met determines our level of happiness. We all have needs but some seem more important to us than others. When your needs are not met, are you left with a deep ache inside which you associate with loneliness?

How we handle our needs is vital. Often we are frightened of our needs, and of seeing them face to face, because experience tells us that they are never met. Instead we believe they get us into trouble or they cause deep pain. Because of this we lock them away and try to carry on with life as though nothing is wrong. When they emerge they are fed by impulse and yet feeding them still seems to leave us hungry. We wonder why there is a kind of hollowness inside us.

Needs don't get met by pushing them down, ignoring them or by covering them up. Our deepest inner needs can only be met by God, whilst more superficial needs can be met by people. There is something within all of us that wishes it didn't all boil down to our relationship with God, but when we choose to believe that God is the key we will spend time with Him and hear what He says regarding our needs and hurts.

I faced an example of the longing for a need to be met, and to see the solution, as I spent time with God one morning. As I was reading my Bible, a member of my family kept flashing before me in my mind. For several days I had felt pain as I longed for a closer relationship with this person: I had a need to be seen for who I really was rather than an image that had been held for years. My need for this change could have led me to feel very down-hearted or bitter.

Instead God showed me that I am securely loved in Him and although it is natural for me to want a good relationship with this person, it would only come as I handed the situation over to Him. As I began to do that, God showed me how I was being treated in a condescending manner because the powers of darkness were reacting to Christ in me. In a sense I was the only one able to change the situation because I could pray into it.

I recognised what my need was in that particular situation but what are your needs:

- unconditional love?
- affirmation?
- respect?
- protection?
- security?
- worth?
- significance?
- touch?
- care?

Our deepest pain is the pain of not feeling loved. Why? Because our deepest need is for love and so much of our life and well-being seems to depend upon that need being met. Our greatest fear is the fear of not being loved. Nothing can truly take that fear away other than the unconditional love of God, which we all need to receive as a revelation. A head knowledge of the love of God doesn't have the power to give us security and remove fear. A revelation, which comes from deep within our spirit, has the power to transform us.

If our greatest need is for love our greatest need is, in fact, for God, because as 1 John 4:16 points out, 'God is love'. If we want to live in love, we must live in God; if we want to know love, we must know God; if we want greater love, we must know more of God. As we know more of God we experience our needs being met in a deeper way. God longs to meet these needs and to draw us close to Him. He is a God who wants to give us the best. Do not deprive yourself by seeking to get your needs met superficially.

Do you allow God to meet these needs? If not, you need to allow Him to meet them by developing your relationship with Him. As the relationship develops you will come to know God's sufficiency. Because God is first, when others fail you, although you may be sad, you will not be left feeling devastated and empty.

We all need the stability of knowing God is there and that His love doesn't change when there is so much change going on around us. One of the main reasons people hold on to routine and familiar patterns is because to them it feels like an island of stability amidst the chaos of life. But we are called to turn to God for stability, to trust Him.

If you don't know what it's like to trust God in this way, or you don't know where to begin, ask. Jesus said, 'Ask and it will be given to you', so ask God to show you how your needs can be met in your relationship with Him. God's promise to all of us is one of filling us and meeting our needs. 'I am the Lord your God, who brought you up out of Egypt. Open wide your mouth and I will fill it' (Psalm 81:10). God is the only one who can fill us, and when we are needy we don't know satisfaction until we are filled.

Truth

I have loved you with an everlasting love; I have drawn you with lovingkindness.

(Jeremiah 31:3)

Action

1. Search through the Scriptures to find all the passages which relate to God meeting your needs, and hold on to them as promises over your life.
2. When faced with difficult situations where you have a deep need submit it to God and ask Him to show you what to do.
3. Ask God to help you to know His sufficiency in meeting your needs.

22 | NEEDING TO GROW

Not being able to assert yourself, be confident or set boundaries can leave you feeling stunted. Being stunted or inhibited in our growth means that we are taken advantage of and not taken seriously. You can also feel very stunted when you don't believe that your opinions count because you can't interact with others in a healthy way. As a result you feel a nobody or just a somebody on the outside, both of which leave you feeling incredibly lonely.

If you believe your opinions don't count or you find it hard to make decisions then you are easily influenced by others. You find yourself just going along with what others say and do. You end up feeling like a piece of driftwood coming in and going out with the tide. In the midst of a storm you feel thrown around and smashed on the rocks. You hate being in such a state and it only creates an even deeper aloneness, but you can't seem to change.

People often believe that change from being tossed to and fro 'just happens', but it actually occurs as we learn to put certain principles into operation. Let's look at some of the ways we can break free from feelings of inhibition, lack of confidence, non-assertiveness and not being able to set boundaries.

On a spiritual level, the first thing we need to do is to acknowledge that we need God's help and wisdom. In many things in life it can seem as if there's no way out but the Psalms remind us, 'God is our refuge and our strength, an ever-present help in trouble' (Psalm 46:1). Frequently we struggle on our own and leave God out of the picture, instead we need to remember that it's God's power working in us which enables us to change!

Having acknowledged that we need God's help, and having asked Him to start the process of change in us, we must trust God that He will be faithful. His nature is faithfulness and so we have no reason to doubt that in His time He will bring about the change we desire. We also need to draw on God's resources to do the very things we feel unable to do. When faced with situations I have previously feared I begin by standing on God's word and on the knowledge that He is always with me. I can also be confident that He gives me what I need, to face situations, if I call upon Him. Psalm 73:26 says, 'My flesh and my heart may fail, but God is the strength of my heart and my portion for ever'.

When we know God as our strength it has a deep effect upon our confidence and ability to assert ourselves and set boundaries. If we are not going to be 'tossed around' we need to develop these skills. In Christian circles the word 'assertiveness' has been misunderstood and a great many people have not been taught the correct meaning of the word and how to apply it in a godly manner. Assertiveness helps us to communicate more clearly our needs and feelings without being either passive or aggressive. Assertiveness and setting boundaries means being honest. You can't say 'yes' when you mean 'no' and then have to find some deceitful means of escaping what you have said yes to.

What else does assertiveness mean?

- taking responsibility for yourself and for your actions
- not taking responsibility for the feelings and actions of others
- taking time to think things through before saying 'yes'
- saying 'no' when you mean no, saying 'yes' when you mean yes
- having a healthy self-respect
- asking instead of expecting others to guess
- allowing yourself to give and to receive compliments

- allowing yourself to make mistakes without self-condemnation
- recognising and accepting *constructive* criticism and rejecting *destructive* criticism
- acting out of love and not duty
- not allowing yourself to be controlled and manipulated by others
- expressing your feelings without being threatened

Very few people will change drastically overnight to being able to put into operation what previously they were unable to do. For most of us change is a process and involves making choices to take the next step. When we choose to trust God and to 'push' ourselves a little further and consequently do something we would have run from in the past, we actually find that it's not as bad as we thought it would be. Our confidence increases, our trust in God's help deepens and we are well on the way to freedom in these areas! We no longer feel stunted, but able.

Truth

> For the Lord will be your confidence and will keep your foot from being snared.
>
> (Proverbs 3:26)

Action

1. Acknowledge that you can't tackle these issues alone and need God's help.
2. Ask God to give you someone who can model godly communication, confidence and assertiveness.
3. Write out the list of what confidence and assertiveness involves, as you become more aware add to the list. Each day pray that God will help you to put into practice what doesn't come naturally.

23 | TRYING TOO HARD

The Christian life is often wrongly seen as one which involves striving. You strive to get up early and spend time with God, you strive to be obedient, you strive to grow. The more effort you put into things the more you believe you will be seen to be a good Christian. So many people actually misinterpret what striving involves because it's different from simply making an effort or being disciplined. It denotes a pushing of self, usually driven by guilt. God doesn't call us to strive but to follow.

Not only do many of us have a tendency to strive but many of us also have a need to achieve. For some people the need to achieve is taken to an extreme and perfectionism begins to dominate their lives. Perfectionism leads to acute loneliness because whatever you do never seems to be good enough. In your quest for perfection you isolate yourself from others. You end up living a life of always trying to put things right instead of living in the grace and mercy of God. Our acceptance has nothing to do with our own effort or deserving: God loves us and blesses us because of who *He* is, not who *we* are. Our relationship with God is based on what He has done for us, not what we can do for Him.

When we are caught in the trap of striving and perfectionism everything seems like hard work. Jesus did not call people to try harder and to carry their loads. He called them to surrender their loads and allow God to carry them. Jesus said, 'Come to me, all you who are weary and burdened, and I will give you rest. Take my yoke upon you and learn from me, for I am gentle and humble in heart, and you will find rest for your souls. For my yoke is easy and my burden is light' (Matthew 11:28–30).

Striving also indicates a lot of hard work without much result. You are left still wanting. When we come to Jesus, receive His peace and allow Him to carry our burdens, we are left not wanting; we lack nothing, as Psalm 23 tells us.

> The Lord is my shepherd, I shall not want.
> He makes me lie down in green pastures,
> he leads me beside quiet waters,
> he restores my soul.
> He guides me in paths of righteousness
> for his name's sake.
> Even though I walk
> through the valley of the shadow of death,
> I will fear no evil,
> for you are with me;
> your rod and your staff,
> they comfort me.
>
> You prepare a table before me
> in the presence of my enemies.
> You anoint my head with oil;
> my cup overflows.
> Surely goodness and love will follow me
> all the days of my life,
> and I will dwell in the house of the Lord
> for ever.

David, the writer of this psalm, spent his boyhood as a shepherd. At the time that he wrote the psalm he was fleeing from his enemies, wandering from place to place. This is what we can be like when we are striving: running from place to place, person to person, looking, wanting and feeling as if we are trapped. David's life was continually being threatened, and when we feel threatened we end up striving to break free, rather than letting God lead us into freedom, as our shepherd.

The shepherd knows and cares for each one of his sheep and their protection is found in the trust of the shepherd. This is the place we need to get to in order confidently to say, 'I shall not want'. Being in that place of 'I shall not want' is being in a place of not striving.

The words 'not want' not only mean not lacking, not being deficient and receiving good care; they also indicate complete contentment and not desiring more. When we are striving or stuck in perfectionism things never satisfy. God is saying if you allow me to be your shepherd and if you will trust me completely you will have no need to strive and no desire for more.

David goes on to say that the shepherd makes him lie down in green pastures. Lying down means resting. When you understand the nature of sheep you see that what David was stating about God was even more significant. Apparently sheep will not lie down unless various criteria are present. They must be free from fear, conflict with other sheep, parasites, flies and hunger.

We too need to be at rest. Like sheep, in order to be at peace inside, we too must be free from fear, friction and tension with others, irritants and distractions and things which suck the life out of us. We must also be free from hunger which means we must be constantly filled spiritually.

If you have found yourself striving recently, either to overcome loneliness or for any other reason, stop for a moment. Spend time quietly before God seeking His peace. Let your body and your mind rest and see God take you by the hand and guide you. It's better to wait for the shepherd to show you the way than to wander off on your own and get lost. Proverbs 20:3 says, 'It is honourable for a man to stop striving' (NKJ).

Truth

Be still before the Lord and wait patiently for Him ...
(Psalm 37:7)

Action

1. Spend time thinking about the areas you are striving in. Begin to see how each of these is like a sheep wandering off on its own.
2. Commit yourself to allowing God to be your shepherd who will guide you and lead you.
3. If you continually find striving a problem bring each of your situations or burdens to God and allow Him to deal with them. Learn to rest in God by seeing that it's not up to you to find the answers.

24 | VICIOUS CIRCLES

One of the frightening things about the state of loneliness is the feeling that in your attempts to be free you end up going round and round in circles. Have you ever seen a hamster in an exercise bubble? He is placed in a clear plastic ball and as he walks the ball goes round, moving across the room. It's a convenient way of containing the hamster whilst allowing him to get plenty of exercise. If the ball were placed on a slight incline the hamster would sense it rolling faster and move more quickly to try to escape the situation. The faster he runs, the faster the ball rolls. He is caught in an ever-increasing cycle!

When we go round and round feeling as if there's no change we get caught in a vicious circle which is usually as a result of a chain reaction. The chain reaction may be different for each one of us, but it basically has the same consequence of getting nowhere and creating a feeling of hopelessness. If I explain a chain reaction I had at one stage in my life it may help you identify your chain reaction.

1. I felt lonely and empty inside →
2. This led to a desire to be cared for →
3. In order to feel cared for I developed manipulative patterns of behaviour →
4. The patterns of behaviour became addictive →
5. Because the patterns were addictive and involved deception and unreality I did not connect with people →
6. Without connecting with people I felt lonely and empty.

That was the scenario in its simplest form. I reasoned, bargained, prayed, made vows to stop and did virtually everything I could but nothing would break the pattern. If you look more closely at what was really going on underneath, at the spiritual level, you can see why my own attempts to change could never have worked.

1. God was not first in my life and so my emptiness was not filled →
2. I desired to be cared for by others more than I desired God →
3. Because of my desire to be cared for I did not seek God's truth →
4. Because my patterns were contrary to God's ways Satan got a hold of me →
5. Drawn into Satan's territory I operated more and more from a position of darkness →
6. Being in darkness my emptiness increased but because I still did not choose God's order my cycle continued.

The most effective way of being free from the cycle is to make sure that it has the correct beginning. I only saw freedom from my patterns of addictive behaviour and deep loneliness when:

1. I chose God to be first in my life and I knew that my deep inner needs could only be met by Him.
2. I desired God, and to be in the right place with Him, more than I desired care and affirmation from others. This meant spending time with Him, trusting Him and worshipping Him.
3. I saw that if I chose God to be first I must choose to believe His truth. I could only believe His truth if I knew His truth, which meant reading the Bible and applying it to everyday situations.
4. I grew to hate Satan and his ways to such an extent that I didn't want him to be a part of my life. This meant not

even entertaining, let alone carrying out, patterns of thinking and behaviour which are contrary to God's ways.

5. Not wanting anything to do with Satan, I chose spiritually to be cut free from the hold he had over me. To keep my freedom meant to keep away from his devices.

6. Choosing God and His ways on a daily basis resulted in my becoming more deeply filled. Emptiness was no longer a part of me and hence I had no need to find my own means of filling it.

If you are in that place now of seeing your loneliness as a vicious circle, and you have not had the revelation of what's going on underneath, then ask God for wisdom. James 1:5 says, 'If any of you lacks wisdom, he should ask God, who gives generously to all without finding fault, and it will be given to him'. Until you know what the real issues are then you don't know what to implement in order to change the cycle. You can still make a start by simply calling out 'Jesus'. Jesus is the name of salvation which means healing and deliverance. Do you want healing and deliverance from your cycle which is self-perpetuating? As you call out to Jesus see His hand stretching out to you. He will take your hand and guide you through your difficulties and hurts which seem beyond change. If you don't call upon the name of Jesus at this stage you can become blinded by the panic of feeling and believing you will remain in the loneliness trap for ever.

I'm sure you have seen a rabbit in the dark dazed by headlights at the roadside. Normally the rabbit would know how to get back from one side of the road to the other. But the car lights dazzle him and leave him paralysed, unable to go in either direction. When we don't see our state of loneliness coming to an end our panic can cause us confusion, and we keep going round and round in circles. We don't know which way to turn; we even lose sight of the concept of choice.

For the rabbit to move again and find his freedom the quickest way is for the car to turn off its headlights. In the same way the quickest way for us to tackle our loneliness is to switch off our panic button. Rather than panic about when you will be free, call on the name of Jesus and then start to break down your route to freedom in manageable stages.

In order to do this think through the areas of your life which you can begin to change. Write you own list, but the following may give you some ideas:

- openness and communication
- expressing your feelings
- socialising with people who encourage you and allowing them to know the 'real' you
- going to church or changing the church you attend
- becoming involved in some form of giving of your time
- changing your living accommodation if it's a part of your loneliness
- speaking positively and not negatively about yourself or life
- having a long-term vision or goal
- allowing yourself 'fun time'
- asking God to show you someone who can disciple you
- not getting overtired, as things get out of perspective

I found the concept of breaking down the areas I need to change very helpful when trying to deal with my own loneliness. As I understood that my loneliness consisted of various factors, such as my inability to communicate and not being able to give of myself, I could then address these areas individually. Each area where change was introduced or where there was growth brought me closer to being free from the state of loneliness.

The important thing is not to panic that you will never

be free, but to take one step at a time and trust God. Remember, the less you panic and the more you learn to submit things to God, even if you don't know how, the more change is going to take place.

Truth

Before they call I will answer; while they are still speaking I will hear.

(Isaiah 65:24)

Action

1. Write a list of the true cycle behind your loneliness.
2. Start to call out the name 'Jesus' in order to switch off your panic button.
3. Look at the areas of your life where you can begin to implement change. Any areas you know you need to change, but feel powerless to do so, submit to God.

25 | THE BARRIERS WE BUILD

When we have been hurt we learn to put up defences to survive in a world full of pain. The defences, also known as coping mechanisms, can work well in shielding us from pain, but can themselves create other problems.

Many of the defences are so subtle that we're unaware of how we use them and how they're wrong in the eyes of God. Sometimes we know that we put them into operation, and we are equally aware of the wrongness of them, but we feel unsure what else to do. Let's look at some of the more common defences and why they are harmful.

1. Denial.

This involves an attempt to minimise the impact of painful situations by refusing to acknowledge them or by not facing up to reality. Saying to people that you're not lonely and then filling that loneliness by comfort eating is a form of denial.

Denial is harmful because it can involve outright dishonesty. We are not only dishonest with others, but frequently with ourselves too. Dishonesty is merely a form of lying and lying is not acceptable to God. Our relationship with God, and with others, must be based on truth. One of the problems with dishonesty is that you have to keep on being dishonest in order to keep up the pretence that everything is OK. You end up living your life in a world of pretence, and as people relate to the image you portray, you remain lonely on the inside.

2. *Suppression.*

This involves burying pain, difficult memories or unacceptable thoughts, in the subconscious. In many ways it's similar to denial except that instead of denying something exists, you constantly push it down. Anger is an emotion which is easily suppressed. Believing it's wrong to be angry, or being frightened to show the emotion, can easily result in our pushing it down. Suppression is harmful because what we suppress doesn't simply disappear – it gets pushed down in one form and re-emerges in another. Instead of feeling angry we become withdrawn or develop physical symptoms.

3. *Regression.*

This involves going back to feeling and behaving like a child. When we look to other adults to 'parent us', or when we don't take responsibility for ourselves and our actions, we can be said to be in a state of regression. Regression is not only harmful to us but also to other people. It's harmful to us because others will often withdraw and not respect us when are an adult but behaving like a child. It's harmful to other people because we often manipulate them in order to receive the response of a loving 'parent'. Manipulation means always twisting things around for our benefit and not the benefit of others, and is therefore violating God's command to love as we are loved by God.

4. *Projection.*

This is when we blame our feelings on other people because it's less painful and avoids personal responsibility. For instance, we say that someone is angry with us when in fact we're unable to admit that we are angry with them. As children of God we are expected to take personal responsibility, and shifting the blame on to someone else is a form of deception. Deception is dangerous because it opposes the truth and is a part of Satan's strategy. Psalm

32:2 says 'Blessed is the man ... in whose spirit is no deceit'.

We have looked at some of the ways we protect ourselves but none of them in the long term bring growth or change, because we are relying on our own devices and not trusting God. This doesn't mean that we should go through life unprotected – quite the opposite. Scripture tells us: 'Above all else guard your heart, for it is the well-spring of life' (Proverbs 4:23). Our hearts need guarding because God knows how delicate they are. But they should not be guarded by our own means, which so often displace God from the centre of our lives. Instead they must be guarded by our trust in the One who created us.

The first few chapters of Proverbs very much emphasise the necessity of following God and not our own means of protection. In chapter 1 we see the implications of independence from God:

> Since they hated knowledge
> and did not choose to fear the Lord,
> since they would not accept my advice
> and spurned my rebuke,
> they will eat of the fruit of their ways
> and be filled with the fruit of their schemes.
> For the waywardness of the simple will kill them,
> and the complacency of fools will destroy them;
> but whoever listens to me will live in safety
> and be at ease, without fear of harm.
>
> (Proverbs 1:29–33)

Self-protection arises out of our trusting ourselves more than we trust God. The book of Proverbs is a book of wisdom on how to conduct our lives, telling us to pay close attention to God's words and to keep them within our hearts.

> My son, pay attention to what I say;
> listen closely to my words.
> Do not let them out of your sight,
> keep them within your heart;
> for they are life to those who find them
> and health to a man's whole body.
>
> (Proverbs 4:20–22)

The reason we are told to pay close attention to God's words and His ways is because they are our life, health and protection from harm. We must keep our eyes continually on God, not looking to other people or things. People may be a part of our protection but they must never take the place of God. We must come to God, be honest concerning how we feel, and share our pain. He is our shield and our protection. We have no need to deny or suppress our feelings because God will never leave us and will always protect us. We can be mature and take personal responsibility by our trust in Him.

Truth

> ... in all your ways acknowledge him, and he will make your paths straight.
>
> (Proverbs 3:6)

Action

1. Examine your life for the ways in which you protect yourself.
2. Choose to lay down your own means of protecting yourself.
3. Walk in God's protection by believing and acting on His word.

26 | RESPECT YOURSELF

Behind so many people's loneliness is a dissatisfaction with self and even, for some, a hatred of self. Yet the ironic thing is that despite wanting to be rid of ourselves, we end up focusing on ourselves far more than people who have a healthy self-respect!

As children of God we are both to love our neighbours as ourselves (Leviticus 19:18) and to deny ourselves (Luke 9:23). This shows that we are to have a respect for ourselves and yet not focus upon ourselves: we are called to have a love *for* ourselves but not a love *of* self. It's wrong to put ourselves down, just as it's wrong to raise ourselves up! Putting ourselves down is dismissing the power of the cross; focusing on ourselves is idolatry!

Instead we are called to live as radical Christians. People think of radical Christians as Christians who are 'over the top' but in fact the word 'radical' refers to the 'root'. The root of Christianity is surrendering self to the cross; it is acknowledging that as a result of the fall, mankind is separated from God and that the only way back is through dying to self and allowing Jesus to reign in us.

To overcome loneliness we must have an accurate picture of ourselves which is based on Jesus and the new life He has given us. If we have a wrong perception such as dissatisfaction with or hatred of self, we act according to that wrong perception which has consequences for our feelings, relationships and most aspects of everyday living. The dissatisfaction with ourselves usually arises from the fact that we believe we are a failure, not good enough, unrighteous and unworthy of drawing close to God.

The only way we can truly be free from feelings of unworthiness and unrighteousness, and so free from disliking ourselves, is to understand how the blood of Jesus changes us. Imagine that even though you are not particularly attractive you are entered for a beauty contest. You dislike yourself so much that you can't even bear the thought of the judge looking at you. Then imagine the judge looking at you through a filter which takes away your plain look, along with all your failings and wrongdoings. The filter causes the judge to see you as a most beautiful person, without a single blemish. The judge turns to you and encourages you to look at yourself through the filter. You search for all your ugliness and wrongdoing but can see none. You can't hate yourself any longer because all the aspects of yourself which you would have classed as being worthy of hatred have been changed into something new. The judge tells you to keep looking at yourself through the filter because without it you see your old self, and not your new self.

The filter is the blood of Jesus. Let's look at how significant the blood is, both in the Old and in the New Testament, in terms of how God sees us. The Old Testament is a shadow of things to come in the New Testament. It showed the people what to look for in the coming of the Messiah. In 1 Samuel 6:19 we read how 50,070 men were struck dead because they looked into the Ark of the Lord. The Ark (which represented God's holy presence) was placed in the Holy of Holies within the Tabernacle (the place where people worshipped God). The Ark itself was a small acacia box, covered in gold, the lid of which was known as the Mercy Seat. Inside the Ark was the Law and once a year the High Priest, who was the only person allowed into the Holy of Holies, would bring the blood of a perfect animal and sprinkle it on the Mercy Seat. Effectively, the blood was being sprinkled between God's holy presence and the Law. When God looked down He didn't judge the people by how well they had kept the Law but rather by the blood covering their sins.

In the same way the blood of Jesus which was shed for us stands between us and God, and so despite our failings enables us to come right into the presence of God. Only when we come into His presence do we experience Him meeting our innermost needs. We all need to pray that we will know what a difference the blood of Jesus makes to our lives and our self-acceptance. A revelation of the blood causes us to want to come close to God, despite our imperfections. The more we take our eyes off our failure and direct them to the wonder of the blood the more we are able to:

- overcome our failure
- walk in righteousness
- accept ourselves
- see freedom from loneliness

We don't need to concentrate on trying to get rid of self-hatred; instead we need to concentrate on the blood of Jesus which has given us a new self, a self which has right standing before God. When we do this we can't hate or be dissatisfied with ourselves. Trying to accept ourselves, to be free from loneliness and to be a better person will never work because trying belongs to the Law. God knew we could never keep the Law and so Jesus' blood was poured out, just as the blood was sprinkled on the Mercy Seat to bridge the gap between our failure and God's holiness. We now live in God's grace.

When we understand the blood we understand our position in Christ – our righteousness. We no longer have to work harder but instead receive what Jesus has done. When we understand righteousness we can understand the word of God and respond to it. When we receive by grace, we don't endeavour to do things in our own strength but rather through the Holy Spirit. The Holy Spirit guides us in all righteousness, convicting us when we are wrong. Until I had a revelation of the blood and understood my righteousness I despised the word 'repentance'; now it is like honey to me because I know the incredible feeling of freedom and right standing it brings.

If you have not received a revelation of the blood, when you hear parts of the word of God (namely obedience, rebuke and discipline) then you feel guilty: 'I'm not good enough'. Once you have received a revelation you know that the focus is not on you but on the blood and so you feel restored.

Remember it's not the *theology* of the blood which will set you free but the *revelation* of the blood; not the knowing *about* the blood but the *putting into practice* the implications of the blood.

Have you said goodbye to the old self who tries hard to keep the Law, and who has a hatred of self for not being good enough? Have you welcomed the new self who, covered in the blood of Jesus, can come into the presence of God at all times? Your new self doesn't have to try harder, but simply receive Jesus and believe that you are a new creation, drawing upon the power of the Holy Spirit to live out that new life.

Truth

... through Christ Jesus the law of the Spirit of life set me free from the law of sin and death.

(Romans 8:2)

Action

1. Develop an understanding of the power of the blood, studying both the Old and the New Testament.
2. Pray for a revelation of the blood and keep praying

until you know without any doubt that you have received the revelation.

3. Praise God that by His grace you are righteous. Now approach Him from that standpoint of righteousness, not from a distorted image of yourself.

27 | YOU AND THE COMMUNITY

Is closing the door for you a painful experience and one associated with loneliness? By 'closing the door' I mean not in a spiritual or emotional sense, but in a very practical way. When you walk through the door, be it your own house, a flat or a room, and close that door behind you, do you fear a crippling aloneness?

Your own home, which is meant to be a place of safety and comfort, can become a place of solitary confinement. You feel alone, eat alone and you watch TV alone. Even if you share the house with other people you can still feel equally alone. Because you feel so confined you focus more and more on how you feel. When you are on your own there is no one to concentrate on but yourself. Your fear of being alone is like a vacuum which sucks you into the inward trap. But when you look inside all you see is more aloneness. The answer isn't to understand why you feel the way you do (this only creates an even deeper look inside) but to begin to look in an outward direction. Two ways which you may find helpful are to develop:

1. A giving heart.
2. A sense of community.

1. *Develop a giving heart.*
When I worked in publishing I remember the title of one book really catching my eye: *Me, myself & I*. None of us likes to admit it but the state of loneliness puts 'me' at the centre of our attention, even if it's merely focusing on how to be free from loneliness. With a lot of pain, no answers

and a deep sense of need, we end up seeing ourselves as needing to receive.

One of the interesting things about biblical principles is that they so often seem to ask us to do the very opposite of what *we* think is best for ourselves. Receiving is no exception to this rule. Jesus says, 'Give, and it will be given to you' (Luke 6:38) and 'It is more blessed to give than to receive' (Acts 20:35).

When we approach life with the attitude of 'What can I give?', rather than 'What can I receive?' we begin to develop a giving heart. If you always think about what you can receive it means seeing yourself as someone in need; if you always think about what you can give it puts you in the position of seeing the richness inside you.

Start to see yourself as a giver. As you give, you will see that others give back in return and your relationship with them changes. No longer do you feel so alone or separate but you make stronger connections with people. You may be lacking in confidence and feeling a little 'low' but you give to someone by a smile, as they pass by, and they respond. The smile develops into a friendly chat. Your giving, through your smile, led to interaction and warmth and added to your learning to relate to others. The alternative would have been to wait for someone to smile, but what if they, seeing your averted gaze – both mentally and physically – avoided you? You would have remained alone, but now disappointed and disillusioned too.

'How can I give when I have nothing to give?' You may be asking yourself this very question. We all have something to give. It's just that some of us find giving more difficult than others. Maybe you feel too embarrassed to say 'Hello' or start a conversation. We will not become more giving people by waiting until we feel more able to give; the only way we become more giving is by beginning to give. Like most things, giving is a skill which we have to choose to do, and gradually work on.

There are so many ways we can give:

- being friendly
- initiating conversation
- writing a letter
- doing something practical for others
- financially supporting people in need
- sacrificing our time for others

Knowing that it's more blessed to give than to receive doesn't mean that we hide behind our giving and then never receive. We must receive too, but when we have received it is not the time to store up what we have like a squirrel preparing for winter. It's the time to give even more. Jesus said, 'Freely you have received, freely give' (Matthew 10:8).

2. *Develop a sense of community.*
In many ways this grows out of a giving heart. When you have a giving heart you interact with others. Developing a sense of community involves being part of a group of people who interact. God has not called us to live in isolation but to share our lives with other people. He has also called believers to be a part of a spiritual body within a fellowship or church.

Sometimes we forget that we are called to be one body in Christ. 1 Corinthians 12:12 reminds us that we are one body, but many parts, 'The body is a unit, though it is made up of many parts; and though all its parts are many, they form one body ...' A sense of belonging and recognising our part within a Christian body is essential. We also have to remember that we don't go to church merely to see what we can get out of the service; we are a part of a body and each part has a function – therefore we have something to give. Church is a lonely place when we are passive. It's also very lonely when we sever ourselves from the body. One of the most common reasons for

severing ourselves from the body is because we've been
hurt by other members and we don't see them as allowed
to have faults. Instead we cut ourselves off and hence
become isolated. Imagine a hand severed from an arm!
The hand has no function on its own; likewise each part of
the body needs the other parts.

As well as being part of a church community on
Sundays we are called to be a part of the community all
the time. Jesus' disciples ate with Him, talked, walked and
learned to communicate with Him. As they related to Him
they grew and changed and their lives were enriched.
After He died those who followed Him met together regularly and shared their lives – their coming together was
not just on the Sabbath. In the same way, beside our relationship with Jesus, we should have close relationships
with one another and be a part of each other's lives.

We all need to find a core group of people (some of
whom will be more mature than we are in our faith) to
whom we can relate and develop a sense of community
living. For some people this actually includes sharing
accommodation or living in close proximity; for others it
may mean living a little distance away and visiting one
another when possible.

Stop for a minute and review your life. Do you tend to
be inward looking? Do you wish to receive more than to
give, and do you keep yourself from others? Do you want
people to respond to you positively and be a part of your
life? If so, are you prepared to ask for God's help in the
areas which may not come very naturally?

Begin to think through ways in which you can give
where previously you wouldn't have done. Look particularly at giving which involves interaction with others.
Think about whether you are committed to a church and
whether you see yourself as a part of the body, with a
function. Think, too, about whether you are a part of a
smaller group. Jesus had 12 disciples, three of whom He
was close to, and one who described himself as 'the one

whom Jesus loved'. We often need a group of people we can relate to but one or two especially close friends we can share everything with. Ask God to give you such people, but be committed to being open and honest, giving and receiving within the relationships.

Truth

> Let us not become weary in doing good, for at the proper time we will reap a harvest if we do not give up.
> (Galatians 6:9)

Action

1. Remind yourself that God created you to relate to others.
2. Start to pray for a heart which longs to give to others.
3. Ask God to show you who the people are you need to develop a close friendship with, and whether you need to make any changes as to where you live in relation to those people.

28 | SURRENDER TO JESUS

Imagine longing to go to the desert to escape the cold weather. You arrive and commit yourself to staying there but in no time you are disillusioned with the vast expanse of sand and feelings of aimlessness. You can see, in the distance, other people who have come to the desert who are enjoying themselves, have food and are basking in an oasis.

In our Christian lives we can wander aimlessly around the desert if we don't move from a place of commitment to daily surrender. Many people commit their lives to Jesus but aren't shown that following on from making a commitment there has to be surrender. Commitment and surrender are two different things: whilst commitment is only our *words*; surrender shows itself through our *actions*. Commitment is acknowledging Jesus as Lord, but surrender is following Jesus each day.

When we read of the first disciples in Matthew, we see more clearly what is meant by following Jesus:

As Jesus walked beside the Sea of Galilee, he saw two brothers, Simon called Peter and his brother Andrew. They were casting a net into the lake, for they were fishermen. 'Come, follow me', Jesus said, 'and I will make you fishers of men'. At once they left their nets and followed him.

Going on from there, he saw two other brothers, James son of Zebedee and his brother John. They were in a boat with their father Zebedee, preparing their nets.

Jesus called them, and immediately they left the boat and their father and followed him.

(Matthew 4:18–22)

The key to understanding a life of surrender is in the words 'follow' or 'followed'. The New Testament Greek word used is 'akoloutheo'. The word can be associated with following Jesus in response to His call on individuals, as opposed to His call to the general crowd. For an individual to follow Jesus involves an abiding fellowship with Him. It means to trust, obey and, in the old terminology, to 'cleave to'. Cleaving to means following His teaching and lifestyle. It speaks of self-denial and fellowship with Jesus.

I think the word 'cleave' is a very meaningful word if you are lonely because it means to adhere or stick close or fast to. We are called to stick close to Jesus. In order for us to overcome a state of loneliness we need closeness, which is really the opposite of loneliness. In loneliness we feel very much on our own; in closeness we are very much a part of another.

How do we surrender our life to Jesus? By choosing Him to be an integral part of us, and choosing to cleave to Him each day. What does that mean in practice? It means knowing that Jesus is the most essential aspect of life and telling Him that we love him. It means giving Him the control of our life because we trust Him. It also means wanting to stick close to His teaching that from the reading of His word (the Bible) obedience grows in our life.

In my own life I find surrender has to start at the beginning of the day. As I am waking, I give my life and that day to God and declare that He is Lord, He is mighty and full of glory.

My next stage of surrender is moving from a place of declaration to a place of action. This involves praying, talking to Jesus as my closest friend and reading God's word. Again this is a daily thing as we can't live off yesterday's food and it is the word of God which feeds us. Joshua 1:8 says, 'Do not let this Book of the Law depart from your mouth; meditate on it day and night, so that you may be careful to do everything written in it. Then you will be prosperous and successful'.

God's words will not be life to us and health to our bodies unless we choose to believe them. I have come to learn that surrender means choosing to believe and applying God's word to my life. Sometimes it can be hard to do this, and we don't think we can believe. For instance, if we don't have much confidence or self-respect it doesn't always come naturally to declare God's unfailing love for us. Yet God's word is that He loves us with an everlasting love. At that point surrender means choosing God's word over our own thoughts and feelings. If we want freedom from loneliness, insecurity and emotional ups and downs, what we believe must come into line with what God says. If we don't do this we are like a double-minded person saying that Jesus is Lord but doing our own thing. As James points out, a double-minded man is unstable in all his ways (see James 1:8).

Why is it so destructive if we don't believe what God says? I believe it's because it displaces God and puts us in His place. It's natural for mankind to want to be in control but being in control, above God, is dangerous. It was this desire to be in control which led to Satan being hurled out of heaven! Isaiah tells us of Satan's downfall, 'You said in your heart, "I will ascend to heaven; I will raise my throne above the stars of God; I will sit enthroned on the mount of assembly ... I will make myself like the Most High". But you are brought down to the grave, to the depths of the pit' (Isaiah 14:13–15).

If we don't follow God every step of the way we are not letting Him be God. This takes me on to my final stage of surrender.

Lastly, in my mind and often aloud, I give God the control over my life that day. In many ways this is the hardest aspect of daily surrender because self loves to go its own way! In each situation where we want to take the control back we need to pray as Jesus prayed 'not my will, but yours be done' (Luke 22:42). I believe that as we give God the control we no longer wander around aimlessly in the desert, nor panic that nothing is in sight. We know that we have a good God and where there is a need for water He leads us to an oasis!

Truth

> The precepts of the Lord are right, giving joy to the heart. The commands of the Lord are radiant, giving light to the eyes.
>
> (Psalm 19:8)

Action

1. If you have made a commitment but have not surrendered your life to Jesus tell Him that you are sorry and ask Him to forgive you. Now make the choice to surrender.
2. Ask God to show you what daily surrender means for you and whether you need to make any changes in your life.
3. Pray as Jesus prayed: 'not my will, but yours be done'.

29 | DOING AWAY WITH FEAR

Fear can be one of those crippling emotions that we never seem to lose. It can have such a firm grip on our lives that we become too frozen and helpless to do or say anything to change a situation.

God doesn't want us to have fear in our lives because it's contrary to His word. The Bible constantly tells us to 'fear not' and 1 John 4:18 says 'perfect love drives out fear'. We need to get to being so secure in God's love that fear cannot get a foothold. So what is fear and why does it have such a powerful hold over our lives?

Fear is an intense emotion often experienced when our well-being is threatened. What do you do when this happens? You want to hide, run or escape. You feel trapped and even immobilised. Someone once summarised fear by describing it as:

False
Expectations
Appearing
Real

If I had to describe what fear felt like and summarise it in a similar form I would say it is:

Feeling
Excessive
Adrenaline
Rush

Most of us are not born full of fear; we develop fears through experiences of deprivation as children, or other painful experiences. Lack of unconditional love is a major cause of fear. Fear restricts our growth as individuals because it prevents us from reaching our potential. Fear also causes damage to our health because the excessive rush of adrenaline exhausts the adrenal glands. Often the illnesses we fear are the very ones we bring upon ourselves.

Fear is a thief which robs us of life and health and instead keeps us captive to its tune of 'what if...'. What are some of the fears you may be experiencing in relation to loneliness?

- isolation
- emptiness
- being left out
- failure
- being rejected
- not relating
- not being understood
- not being accepted
- not being valued
- losing friends
- intense emotion
- being vulnerable
- trusting people
- communicating
- losing out in life
- being ill
- not being able to share

What can you do to overcome your fears?

1. *Know what your fears are and where they come from.*
Start to become familiar with your fears so that you're not living in denial of their existence. Ask yourself whether

there is any reason behind what you fear and whether it's rational or irrational.

2. *Surrender your fears to God and receive His unconditional love.*

Surrender brings release. When we hear God say to us 'Fear not' and we respond in faith then we receive a deliverance from our fears. Responding in faith is receiving the unconditional love of God. We need a revelation of God's love for us, and we need to thank and praise God for his love for us in order to see fear go. As we do this we are both allowing a 'renewing of the mind' to take place and we are 'taking every thought captive to the obedience of Christ'. Taking every thought captive involves believing that the unconditional love of God is more powerful than the fear of man.

Proverbs 29:25 says, 'Fear of man will prove to be a snare, but whoever trusts in the Lord is kept safe'. A high percentage of our fears have to do with the fear of man – for instance, fear of being hurt and rejected and fear of what others think. As Proverbs points out, to fear man is to walk into a snare which is a trap or place of bondage. How do we avoid walking into the snare? By trusting God. You can trust God, by knowing what He is like:

> He will cover you with his feathers,
> and under his wings you will find refuge;
> his faithfulness will be your shield and rampart.
> You will not fear the terror of night,
> nor the arrow that flies by day,
> nor the pestilence that stalks in the darkness,
> nor the plague that destroys at midday.
>
> (Psalm 91:4–6)

3. *Take authority over the stronghold of fear.*

Fear can become a stronghold in our lives. A stronghold is basically a hold of the enemy. Negative patterns of thought become deeply ingrained in our minds through repeated patterns or traumatic experiences. You reach a stage where you automatically act according to the stronghold, and trying to change makes no difference. Because that pattern has become a hold of Satan's, it only changes when the stronghold is commanded to come down in the name of Jesus, when a believer takes authority over the stronghold. After you have taken authority over the stronghold there needs to be the renewing of the mind: that is filling the mind with God's truth. When you experience the difference between a life full of fear and a life free from fear you have no desire for fear to be a part of you. Ask God to give you an overwhelming desire to be fear-free, and to realise that you will overcome your fears because Jesus is bigger than any of them!

Truth

> Do not fear, for I am with you; do not be dismayed, for I am your God.
>
> (Isaiah 41:10)

Action

1. Write a list of all your fears and commit them to God, asking Him to show you His unconditional love.
2. Realise that overcoming your fears means commanding in the name of Jesus that the strongholds come down, and taking every thought captive to the obedience of Christ.
3. Always make sure that Jesus is bigger in your mind than your fears are. As you focus on Him allow your mind to be renewed by going over and over the truth of who Jesus is to you and what he has done for you.

30 | RECOGNISING THE ENEMY

Imagine being blind. It's broad daylight, the sun is shining, people are walking around and you can see nothing. You are in the world yet don't know what it looks like. As you walk along you bump into things which you can't see. They hinder your walk but you don't always know what they are or how to get around them. You think 'if only my eyes could be opened'.

Being in the dark can be frightening and most of us prefer to switch on a light to see what is what. Generally when you are in the dark, you know how to get into the light: when you enter your home in the evening the first thing you reach for is the light switch. You have to choose to switch on the light to dispel the darkness.

Have you ever thought about what you believe regarding light and dark spiritually? To overcome loneliness you need to know about light and dark spiritually and it is essential that you know how to get rid of darkness. Do you believe in Satan and his forces, his demons? If you are a Christian do you ever take into consideration that he takes great delight in attacking you? If we don't recognise attack then we will certainly not do anything to combat it. Attack is Satan's way of trying to undermine, pull down and destroy God's people. How does he attack us? In numerous ways, such as:

- sowing doubt into our minds and questioning God's word
- putting temptation in our way
- causing us to focus on ourselves and not God

- using other people to undermine and criticise us
- feeding us lies about ourselves, others and God
- causing confusion and difficult situations in an attempt to prevent God's work

Not only does Satan use tactics against us, but he tries to lure us into his territory. If we compromise God's word and allow ourselves to do or say things which are contrary to God's ways, we actually give Satan an opening to attack us.

I remember at one period in my life letting a situation of injustice move from anger to bitterness and self pity. It had a snowball effect: anger attracted anger and as the ball of anger continued to roll it picked up other negative emotions along the way. Soon my outlook on life became very pessimistic and my behaviour patterns unacceptable. Because I had allowed my anger to move into unforgiveness I had given the devil a foothold. My emotions and behaviour only changed when I saw in very black and white terms what belonged to God's territory and what belonged to Satan's territory. For instance:

God's territory	Satan's territory
forgiveness	unforgiveness
acceptance	jealousy
affirmation	rejection
patience	abuse
truth	lying
love	hatred
submission	rebellion
self-control	self-indulgence
compassion for others	self-pity
harmony	discord
kindness	malice
gentleness	aggression
trust	fear
faith	doubt

Because Satan's kingdom is a kingdom of darkness, his territory is a place of darkness. When we allow ourselves to step over into his territory there are consequences. It's easy to think that a little unforgiveness or self-pity, for instance, doesn't matter, but we fail to realise that anything in Satan's territory affects us. The longer we spend in his territory the more affected we are, the more in bondage we become.

We have to learn not only to see the two territories in black and white, but to so detest the enemy that we want nothing to do with him. Having nothing to do with him means steering clear of anything which leads to entering his camp.

When Satan does attack us, as he will inevitably try to do, we must be prepared for him and we must fight. In the next chapter we will look at preparing ourselves to overcome in the battle. For the weapons which God has given us are weapons for winning, not losing!

Truth

> Submit yourselves then, to God. Resist the devil, and he will flee from you.
>
> (James 4:7)

Action

1. Recognise that Satan and his forces exist and don't dismiss the fact that he desires to attack you.
2. Make a list of things in your life which you now realise are in Satan's territory. If you mean it, tell God that you are sorry you have allowed yourself to step out of His territory and into that of the enemy.
3. Decide what practical steps you are going to take to remove certain aspects of your life from the enemy's 'hold'. Ask God for wisdom.

31 | *STAND UP AND FIGHT!*

When you are under attack from the enemy in relation to loneliness or any other situation and feel defeated you do not have to be a wounded soldier; you can be a mighty warrior! How? By putting on the armour of God. Ephesians 6 teaches us exactly what the armour is and likens each piece to the outfit of a soldier in biblical times. The armour is something which we need to put on every day. It's no good putting the armour on after you have begun to be attacked. We need to have the armour on at all times; when being attacked it's the time to fight, not to start getting dressed!

> Finally, be strong in the Lord and in his mighty power. Put on the full armour of God so that you can take your stand against the devil's schemes. For our struggle is not against flesh and blood, but against the rulers, against the authorities, against the powers of this dark world and against the spiritual forces of evil in the heavenly realms. Therefore put on the full armour of God, so that you may be able to stand your ground, and after you have done everything, to stand. Stand firm then, with the belt of truth buckled round your waist, with the breastplate of righteousness in place, and with your feet fitted with the readiness that comes from the gospel of peace. In addition to all this, take up the shield of faith, with which you can extinguish all the flaming arrows of the evil one. Take the helmet of salvation and the sword of the Spirit, which is the word of God. And pray in the Spirit on all

occasions with all kinds of prayers and requests.
(Ephesians 6:10–18)

Most of us, if we feel pulled down, low, empty or oppressed, need to do an armour check! Let's look a little more closely at what we should be putting into operation on a daily basis to fend off the enemy and his attacks. We must:

1. *Be strong in the Lord and in His mighty power.*
That means putting our full confidence in God and in His power to save and deliver us. If we have a weak vision of God we will only expect a weak version of His power. We may have no confidence in ourselves because by ourselves we have no power and authority. In Jesus we have power and authority so therefore we must have all confidence in God.

2. *Put on the full armour of God.*
We can't put on only the parts of the armour which we think suit us. We are instructed to put on the *full* armour of God which means that in no way can we be defeatist. Also, when we are all dressed in armour people recognise us – including the enemy – and when they see that we are a part of God's army and that we have all our weapons ready they will think twice before attacking!

3. *Recognise that we are in a spiritual battle and fight with spiritual weapons.*
Begin to see your battles from a spiritual perspective and learn how to wage war spiritually. When you feel depressed or negative do you take authority in the name of Jesus, speak out the word of God or praise God so that your spirit is lifted? Or do you automatically think 'What's wrong with me, I need to talk to someone'? We must win our battles at a spiritual level to have any lasting effect at an emotional level.

4. *Stand firm.*

Standing firm means believing in, and living your life according to, the truth of God's word. When you know the truth you also know what is not truth! We are called to a position of no compromise as believers. Compromise is essentially 'watering down' the Gospel by allowing things to be a part of your life which contradict the word of God. Doubt is also a compromise; we are called to a position of faith and not a position of doubt.

5. *Put on the belt of truth.*

Have you securely fastened around yourself the truth of God's word, His promises and His message to us? We must allow our minds to be filled with the truth. If we don't we lose our position of defence. For instance, if we are told not to have envy and selfish ambition and we harbour these things then we have loosened the belt and are open to attack. 'For where you have envy and selfish ambition, there you find disorder and every evil practice' (James 3:16).

6. *Put on the breastplate of righteousness.*

We must desire righteousness in our lives. Righteousness means a right relationship with God. David, in the Psalms wrote, 'Search me, O God, and know my heart; test me and know my anxious thoughts. See if there is any offensive way in me, and lead me in the way everlasting' (Psalm 139:23–24). It takes courage to say this to God. When was the last time you said to God (and meant it) 'Show me if there is anything within me, even the slightest thought, that is not right in your eyes?' Being in a right relationship with God means doing what is acceptable to Him – and if you 'fall', repenting and coming straight back to Him. Learn to be 'squeaky clean', and in order to do that we must learn what is considered as 'unclean'.

7. *Make sure our feet are fitted with the readiness that comes from the gospel of peace.*

What do you associate with the word 'readiness'? When I think of the word I see 'keenness', eagerness', and 'desire'. We must be eager to share the gospel of peace with others wherever we go.

8. *Take up the shield of faith.*

Faith is our shield and we are not going to get very far in battle without a shield! As soon as we walk by sight and not by faith we drop our shield, so to speak. 'And without faith it is impossible to please God, because anyone who comes to him must believe that he exists and that he rewards those who earnestly seek him' (Hebrews 11:6). Faith says, 'If I trust God, I know that He is with me at all times'. Faith means putting into operation what God says even when we are waiting to see results.

9. *Take the helmet of salvation.*

We not only need to be saved, but to be secure in our salvation. People often make a commitment to Jesus but still doubt salvation. We are told to put on the helmet of salvation and the helmet protects our minds. It also means taking on board all that Christ did for us through His death.

10. *Take the sword of the Spirit.*

The sword of the Spirit is the word of God which we must allow to be etched into our whole being. How would you feel if someone came at you wielding a sharp sword? You would run! The word of God is very powerful as a form of spiritual warfare, it '... is living and active. Sharper than any double-edged sword, it penetrates even to dividing soul and spirit, joints and marrow; it judges the thoughts and attitudes of the heart' (Hebrews 4:12). When Jesus was in the wilderness and tempted by Satan, He did not cast Satan out but spoke the word to him which left Satan powerless to answer back! We need to *know* the word to defend ourselves with the sword.

11. *Pray in the Spirit on all occasions.*

Prayer is vital and we need both to pray in the Spirit and pray on all occasions. Praying in the Spirit is when we listen to the Holy Spirit and pray from our spirit and not from our mind. To fight we need to pray like this on all occasions. We must live a life of continual communion with God.

As you put on the armour each day you will find that your eyes will be opened to know when darkness is descending. Don't ever think that darkness can't be overcome. God is light and as we bring Him into situations we bring light. We must praise and worship God throughout the day. Satan hates us praising God because it exalts God higher than him, and he wants to be first. The more we praise God the less opportunity there is for Satan to 'get hold of us'.

What if Satan does 'get hold of us'? The armour protects us, but we must still fight. Suppose someone was trashing your garden, purposely pulling up the roses, smashing the vegetables and destroying what has taken you many years of care and hard work. No doubt you would feel angry and demand that the person stop and leave your property. We have to do exactly the same with Satan and his demons: proclaim aloud 'In the name of Jesus, I command you to stop'.

If you are in God's army let's work together to see the enemy flee.

Truth

> For though we live in the world, we do not wage war as the world does.

> (2 Corinthians 10:3)

Action

1. Put on the whole armour of God each day, not by *reading* Ephesians 6 but by *doing* Ephesians 6.
2. Realise that you get rid of darkness by keeping the light on! The more we praise God and worship Him throughout the day the less room there is for darkness in our lives.
3. Decide that you are going to fight the devil and not be trampled on by him.

32 | DON'T BE DEFEATED

In the last chapter we looked at the importance of putting on the armour of God to protect ourselves from wounds, knocks, attacks, and outright defeat from the enemy!

In order to be able to put on the armour, and fight, we need to have a comprehensive understanding of our position within the army of God. In any army the people need to know not just that they have the weapons to fight but that they have the authority to go with them. We need to know that we are not going to war to be defeated, but that because we are in a position of authority we are in the best place to win. When you know the authority you operate with confidence. Part of the reason that many Christians don't stand up in battle is that they see themselves as defeated and insignificant so they lack confidence; their lack of confidence comes from not truly knowing the tremendous authority they have as believers.

We don't create our own authority to fight and to overcome the powers of darkness, because we receive the authority from Jesus. We read:

> When Jesus had called the Twelve together, he gave them power and authority to drive out all demons and to cure diseases, and he sent them out to preach the kingdom of God and to heal the sick.
>
> (Luke 9:1–2)

The disciples could not have driven out demons and cured diseases in their own power and strength. In the same way we can stand up against the kingdom of darkness because Jesus' power and authority is at work within us.

Authority is the *right* to rule and power is the *ability* to rule. They go hand in hand. It's no good having the right without the ability and vice versa. If you are a Christian, committed to Jesus, say aloud, 'Because of Jesus I have the power and the authority to overcome the kingdom of darkness; I have the right and the ability to command the enemy to go!' Are you beginning to believe that you no longer have to remain defeated and insignificant? Remember that they are free gifts and not dependent on you. Nor do you have to feel that taking authority will not work for you, because it's Jesus in you that the powers of darkness shrink from, not you as a person. We only have significance, power and authority through the name of Jesus.

As well as understanding and believing that we have the power and authority of Jesus, we must learn to recognise the nature of the enemy's work so that we can exercise that authority in response to it. Often Satan's ways are very subtle. Have you begun to see the pattern in his devices of destruction?

- control and manipulation from other people
- thinking that you are powerless
- being pulled down by cruel words from others
- fear and intimidation
- gossiping and backbiting
- believing you can't hear God

The list is endless and as we begin to view things with our spiritual eyes we will see more and more how important it is to take authority over the spiritual powers at work behind such incidents as mentioned above. We also have to see that when the name and power of Jesus are spoken the powers of darkness will flee, because they have no power against Jesus. We are not stuck in the middle of a war between the kingdom of darkness and the kingdom of light, with both of equal strength. No! 'He who is in you is greater than he who is in the world' (1 John 4:4 NKJ). We will only see Jesus' power at work when we understand the order of creation.

Jesus said, 'All authority in heaven and on earth has been given to me' (Matthew 28:18). It's clear that Jesus is at the top and that because he has given His authority and power to His followers they are underneath Him. Where then are Satan and all his forces? Because he is subject to Christ's authority and we have been given Christ's authority he is under our feet! He was defeated at the cross.

Many Christians wonder why, if Satan has already been defeated and he is under our feet, he still creates so much chaos in our lives? This is because his very nature is to deceive you. He deceives you into believing that you have no power over him and that your struggles in life have nothing to do with him. If someone weak deceives us into believing that they have tremendous power then, in our eyes, they become a giant and we are afraid of them.

If you do not believe that you have authority you do not exercise it. You may be thinking, 'It was all very well for the disciples, they had Jesus, but I can't do as they did'. You can! The disciples were with Jesus, but you and I are *in* Jesus. This means that we have His Spirit operating through us and so we have the same power at work within us.

When you take authority it's not down to how much authority you have, it's how much authority Jesus has and believing that it has been given to you! We are merely Jesus' representatives and when we say that we come in His name the spiritual powers of darkness flee. They may not know who *you* are but they certainly know who *Jesus* is. That's why when we take authority (which is done aloud) we need to do so in the name of Jesus. We will then realise that we can't be defeatist.

Paul wrote in his letter to the Ephesians, 'I pray also that the eyes of your heart may be enlightened in order that you may know the hope to which he has called you, the riches of his glorious inheritance in the saints, and his incomparably great power for us who believe' (Ephesians 1:18–19). Paul realised that the stumbling block for most people was that they had a problem believing their authority and seeing their position in Christ. In the same way we all need to pray for our eyes to be opened if we are to conquer and not be defeated. It's not that some don't have the power at hand whilst others do, but that they don't believe they, personally, have the authority.

If you have not believed you have all authority and power, start today by choosing to receive what you have already been given. As you put it into operation you will be surprised at the difference between feeling defeated and knowing you can conquer.

Truth

... you have been given fullness in Christ, who is the Head over every power and authority.

(Colossians 2:10)

Action

1. Pray that the eyes of your understanding may be opened.
2. Read any passages you can find in the New Testament relating to the power and authority you have, such as Luke 9:1–2; Luke 10:19–20. Then begin the sentence 'I have', for instance, 'I have all authority to trample on snakes and scorpions and to overcome all the power of the enemy'.
3. Start to exercise the authority you have in Jesus as you face the powers of darkness in everyday problems.

33 | BREAKING FREE!

So if the Son sets you free, you will be free indeed.

(John 8:36)

You can't be with Jesus without being changed. But as we have uncovered throughout this book there is an important difference between *knowing* God and *walking* with Him. When you walk with someone you stay close and you are always conscious of their presence. Your being in their presence has an impact upon you and changes you. In the same way if you have applied the word of God whilst reading *Breaking Free From Loneliness* you will have changed. Just as the disciples didn't realise how much they had changed until after Jesus had died, you too may not realise how much you have changed until after you have finished reading this book.

As I summarise some of what has been said in this book I would like to suggest that you take each point and use it as a checklist for your life. See if there are any areas of your life that you now want to adjust. It would be good as the months go by to keep looking over the checklist to see what else you can 'tick off'.

Checklist

1. Be 'born again' by receiving Jesus as your Lord and Saviour.
2. Be baptised and filled with the Holy Spirit, who is your teacher, counsellor and comforter.
3. Make God the centre of your life and your whole being.

4. Praise and thank God on all occasions.

5. Submit your body, soul and spirit to God, so that you may know the difference between acting according to the flesh and acting according to the spirit.

6. Develop a comprehensive understanding of the nature of God.

7. Receive as truth what Jesus has accomplished for you on the cross, knowing that God sees you through Jesus.

8. Live your life knowing that your old nature has been put to death and you are now a new creation.

9. Believe the truth about who you are as God's child and the inheritance which you have received.

10. Be consumed by God and not by your problems.

11. Admit that in your own strength you cannot fight, but that with God all things are possible.

12. Develop honesty with God, yourself and with others.

13. Submit to God any past hurts and receive Jesus as the One who brings healing to your wounds.

14. Abandon your own means of protecting yourself, and find your security in God.

15. Make a conscious decision to forgive on all occasions.

16. Repent of any idols in your life, of pretence, envy and self-pity.

17. Pray for a revelation of the blood of Jesus and the power this has in your life.

18. Pray for a revelation of the unconditional love God has for you and wants you to receive.

19. Live by Jesus' teaching through the reading of the Word and the putting of it into operation.

20. Put on the whole armour of God each day and resist the devil.

21. Believe and exercise the authority you have as a Christian.

22. Take every thought captive to the obedience of Christ and command strongholds to come down in the name of Jesus.

Overcoming the enemy and his tactics for withholding fullness of life from us is worthwhile because God promises great rewards. Revelation 21:6–7 says '… To him who is thirsty I will give to drink without cost from the spring of the water of life. He who overcomes will inherit all this'. Do not ever be content with giving in or taking the easy option. We must not give the devil two punches and call it a day. We must fight and resist until he flees. If that takes two attempts or two hundred attempts it should make no difference. Abraham waited 25 years, following God's promise to him, for the birth of Isaac. At one point he took the easy option and had a son by one of his maids, but it was not the promised child. Never give up on God's promises.

I shall close by quoting from the book of Job. As you read these words ask God to tell you what the relevance of the words are *for you.*

> Submit to God and be at peace with him;
> in this way prosperity will come to you.
> Accept instruction from his mouth
> and lay up his words in your heart.
> If you return to the Almighty, you will be restored:
> if you remove wickedness far from your tent
> and assign your nuggets to the dust,
> your gold of Ophir to the rocks in the ravines,
> then the Almighty will be your gold,
> the choicest silver for you.
> Surely then you will find delight in the Almighty
> and will lift up your face to God.
> You will pray to him and he will hear you,
> and you will fulfil your vows.
> What you decide on will be done,
> and light will shine on your ways.
>
> (Job 22:21–28)

To walk in the truth is to walk in freedom.

Truth

It is for freedom that Christ has set us free. Stand firm, then, and do not let yourselves be burdened again by a yoke of slavery.

(Galatians 5:1)

Action

1. Abide in God's word.
2. Have intimacy with Jesus.
3. Each day ask God to fill you with His Holy Spirit.

Nicholaston House
Christian Healing Centre

The vision for Nicholaston House came about long before it was purchased. Some 13 years prior to the House coming on the market in 1998, a group of Christians in a Methodist Chapel, in a rural location on Gower, began praying for a place where people could get away from the stresses of life to receive help and rest. They believed that God would bring the Centre into being and that their role was to pray for it. Meanwhile a couple in Surrey received a vision for 'a place where people who are hurting could come and find space'. A series of God-ordained events resulted in that couple, Derrick and Sue Hancock, moving to Swansea, becoming involved in Swansea City Mission, and the Mission purchasing Nicholaston House. Other people who now work at Nicholaston House also had similar visions for a residential centre for healing, and hence the House is born out of the prayers, visions and longings of several people who, over the years, have had a heart to see God bring healing and restoration to broken lives.

In the entrance of the House are the words, 'In this place I will give peace'. People frequently comment on the peace they experience during their stay and the ways in which they encounter the presence of God in the House. As well as coming for rest, space and ministry, people come to Nicholaston House to participate in the week and weekend courses and retreats on offer. These events include prayer ministry, time out, creative activities, spiritual encouragement, and insight and support for those addressing a number of personal issues, such as eating disorders.

The location of the House itself is ideal for rest and renewal. Set in the heart of the Gower Peninsula, an area of outstanding natural beauty, Nicholaston House overlooks the stunning Bay of Oxwich with its vast expanse of sand. In contrast, a country lane separates the back of the House from Cefn Bryn, where sheep, ponies and cattle roam free across miles of open moorland. The whole area creates an ambiance of peace and tranquillity.

Inside the House, the downstairs comprises a sea-facing dining room, conservatory and lounge, a craft and bookstall and two medium-sized conference rooms. The conference rooms can be opened up into one large room seating over 100 people.

Upstairs there is a lounge and a small chapel and library, as well as accommodation for around 28 people. All the bedrooms are en-suite (most are twin) and have colour television and tea and coffee making facilities. Many are sea-facing, and a passenger lift, as well as the main staircase, serve all. One bedroom is specifically adapted for those with disabilities – including wheelchair users. The disabled toilets, ramps and lift, make the House available to all.

The gardens, which overlook the sea, are designed to encourage relaxation and the House is a member of the Quiet Gardens Trust.

In order to find out more about the work of Nicholaston House, you can visit the website or write and ask for an information pack (which includes details of the work, in-house events and resources). If you would like your name added to the mailing list, which means you will be kept up-to-date with latest news on events and will receive a bi-annual newsletter, please send a large SAE to:

Nicholaston House, Penmaen, Gower, Swansea SA3 2HL
Tel: 01792 371317 Fax: 01792 371217
Email: managers@nicholastonhouse.org
Website: www.nicholastonhouse.org